Moldova

Poverty Assessment

The World Bank
Washington, D.C.

1-27-00

World Bank Country Studies are among the many reports originally prepared for internal use as part of the continuing analysis by the Bank of the economic and related conditions of its developing member countries and of its dialogues with the governments. Some of the reports are published in this series with the least possible delay for the use of governments and the academic, business and financial, and development communities. The typescript of this paper therefore has not been prepared in accordance with the procedures appropriate to formal printed texts, and the World Bank accepts no responsibility for errors. Some sources cited in this paper may be informal documents that are not readily available.

The findings, interpretations, and conclusions expressed in this paper are entirely those of the author(s) and should not be attributed in any manner to the World Bank, to its affiliated organizations, or to members of its Board of Executive Directors or the countries they represent. The World Bank does not guarantee the accuracy of the data included in this publication and accepts no responsibility for any consequence of their use. The boundaries, colors, denominations, and other information shown on any map in this volume do not imply on the part of the World Bank Group any judgment on the legal status of any territory or the endorsement or acceptance of such boundaries.

The material in this publication is copyrighted. The World Bank encourages dissemination of its work and will normally grant permission promptly.

Permission to photocopy items for internal or personal use, for the internal or personal use of specific clients, or for educational classroom use, is granted by the World Bank provided that the appropriate fee is paid directly to Copyright Clearance Center, Inc., 222 Rosewood Drive, Danvers, MA 01923, U.S.A., telephone 978 750 8400, fax 978 750 4470. Please contact Copyright Clearance Center prior to photocopying items.

For permission to reprint individual articles or chapters, please fax your request with complete information to the Republication Department, Copyright Clearance Center, fax 978 750 4470.

All other queries on rights and licenses should be addressed to the World Bank at the address above, or fax no. 202 522 2422.

ISBN: 0-8213-4477-3
ISSN: 0253-2123

Library of Congress Cataloging-in-Publication Data has been applied for.

CONTENTS

FIGURES

TABLES

BOXES

TOOL BOXES

ABSTRACT

This report is written at the request of the Government of Moldova, which is its primary audience. It aims to provide a detailed analysis of the situation regarding living standards in the country, and provide a framework for policy for the Government's emerging social assistance program.

It draws on data from two surveys: the Moldova Department of Statistics's revised Household Budget Survey, for February (pilot), May and August 1997, and later updates until December 1998, and an ethnographic survey of poor households conducted in November 1996.

Chapter 1 of the report examines the composition and distribution of poverty in Moldova. Chapter 2 looks at how income and price shocks have affected the lives of the poor—and motivates the need for employment-generating growth, especially in agriculture, as the only sure way out of poverty for most Moldovans. Chapter 3 discusses the role of the Moldovan state in easing poverty, and proposes a broad strategy to reform social assistance and social sector reform that best uses the limited Government resources.

This report concentrates on analyzing the results for the Right Bank of Moldova, so that any references to Moldova imply the Right Bank. The technical papers on which this report is based also present evidence for Transnistria. They are in "Moldova: Poverty Assessment Technical Papers," (Report No. 19846 MD, the World Bank, Washington DC). The Technical Papers comprise of a qualitative assessment of Moldovan poverty, poverty profiles of Moldova, a labor market study, and an examination of health and education issues as they relate to the poor in Moldova.

This report was prepared by a team composed of Arup Banerji (team leader), Jeanine Braithwaite (poverty profile and social assistance), Robert Ackland (poverty profile, social assistance and social expenditures), Mikle Peleah (poverty profile update and poverty simulations), David Lindauer (labor markets), Nora Dudwick and Hermine de Soto (ethnographic survey), Elena Nikulina (poverty profile and social assistance). A special thanks to Doreen Duff (coordination and support) for her extensive and cheerful help at all stages of preparing this document. In the final stages of document preparation, Usha Rani Khanna (editing), Victor Guzun (translation) and Matthew Kehn (processing) provided valuable help.

Valuable inputs and suggestions were received from Asad Alam, Mats Anderson, Sue Ellen Berryman, Csaba Csaki, Mark Davis, Carlos Elbirt, Armin Fidler, Christine Jones, Kathleen McCollom, Wlodek Okrasa, James Parks, Ana Revenga,

Maya Sandu, Alan Thompson and Ruslan Yemtsov and Xiaoqing Yu. Nisha Agrawal was the peer reviewer.

The report was written under the general guidance of Roger Grawe and Pradeep Mitra. The sector manager was Hafez Ghanem.

The team would like to express its thanks to the many officials and institutions in the Moldovan Government, as well as those from Moldovan civil society, whose cooperation, comments and inputs made the report possible. In particular, special thanks are due to the Ministries of Economy, Finance, and Labor, Family and Social Protection, the Department of Statistics, and the Center for Strategic Studies in Chisinau.

CURRENCY EQUIVALENTS
(as of July 30, 1997)

Currency Unit	=	Leu (plural Lei)
1 Leu	=	US$0.22
US$1	=	4.60 Lei

(as of May 13, 1999)

Currency Unit	=	Leu (plural Lei)
1 Leu	=	US$ 0.09
US$1	=	10.85 Lei

WEIGHTS AND MEASURES
Metric System

FISCAL YEAR
January 1 - December 31

ABBREVIATIONS AND ACRONYMS

CIS - Commonwealth of Independent States
ECA - Europe and Central Asia
FSU - Former Soviet Union
GDP - Gross Domestic Product
GNP - Gross National Product
IMF - International Monetary Fund
OECD - Organisation For Economic Co-operation and Development
PPP - Purchasing Power Parity
TACIS - Technical Assistance for Commonwealth of Independent States
UNDP - United Nations Development Programme

Vice President:	Johannes Linn (ECAVP)
Country Director:	Roger Grawe (ECC07)
Sector Director:	Pradeep Mitra (ECSPE)
Sector Manager:	Hafez Ghanem (ECSPE)
Task Team Leader:	Arup Banerji (ECSPE)
Team Members:	Jeanine Braithwaite, Elena Nickulina, Doreen J. Duff (ECSPE); Nora Dudwick (ECSSD); Robert Ackland (consultant); Hermine de Soto (consultant); David L. Lindauer, (consultant)

EXECUTIVE SUMMARY

Moldova is having an arduous transition from being a centrally-planned economy to one that is guided by market signals, and this has contributed to poverty. Its agriculture-dominated economy, once thriving, is handicapped today by the loss of its traditional markets and the slow restructuring of its enterprises. As a result, the economy has been shrinking since independence. And, with it, enterprise-based employment and social support structures have eroded as well. This has had two effects on poverty—cash incomes have been lower, due to a stagnant overall labor market, and non-cash transfers and implicit subsidies from enterprises and the Government have been decreasing in Moldova.[1] Poverty, therefore, is significant. Using an absolute poverty line for Moldova of 82.10 lei per person per month (about $220 a year at market exchange rates) in May 1997, 35 percent of Moldovans were poor. Using a relative poverty line (of 40 percent of average consumption) in the same period, 19 percent of the population were "relatively" poor.[2]

The regional crisis in 1998, which helped bring about a sharp decline in Moldova's GDP, has made poverty even greater. Absolute poverty has worsened significantly. Using the same absolute poverty line as in May 1997, 46 percent of Moldovans were poor in the fourth quarter of 1998. In particular, comparing the third and fourth quarters in 1997 to those in 1998, the number of people whose consumption was less than the absolute poverty line have increased sharply (Figure I).

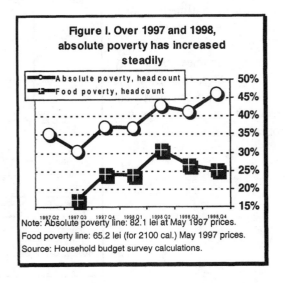

Figure I. Over 1997 and 1998, absolute poverty has increased steadily

Note: Absolute poverty line: 82.1 lei at May 1997 prices.
Food poverty line: 65.2 lei (for 2100 cal.) May 1997 prices.
Source: Household budget survey calculations.

The increase in poverty has been against the backdrop of an increase in inequality. In 1987-88, the Gini coefficient for income inequality was 24 (where zero reflects perfect equality and 100 total inequality). By 1992, it had risen to 34.4 and in 1993, it was 36. The 1997 household survey data finds the Gini for consumption to be about 40, with the richest 20 percent of the population consuming about 4,300 lei ($925) a year, almost half of total consumption in the economy. In urban areas, the gap was larger, with the richest 20 percent consuming about 60

---

[1] Throughout this document, "Moldova" refers to the Right Bank, i.e., the part excluding Transnistria. The technical papers also present evidence for Transnistria.

[2] The quantitative analysis uses data from the Moldova Household Budget Survey, the pilot for which was done in February 1997, with successive rounds in May, August and November 1997, and quarterly since. The data, however, is not a panel, but a sample in each time period. The samples are representative within each quarter and for the entire year.

percent of the total, and the poorest fifth consuming around 3 percent of all consumption. While inequality has worsened, it is still no worse than that in countries such as the Philippines (a Gini of 42.9 in 1994) or Malaysia (a Gini of 48.4 in 1989), and is comparable to those of many countries at Moldova's level of per capita income. It is also comparable to the levels in the region. For example, Georgia, in end-1997, had a Gini of 0.38 for total household consumption. Russia, in 1993, had an income Gini of 0.31 (Table I).

Table I: Comparative distribution of consumption, Moldova and Georgia (Fall 1997) and of incomes, Russia (1993) (% of total)			
	Moldova	**Georgia**	**Russia**
Poorest quintile	6	6	7
2nd quintile	10	12	13
3rd quintile	15	17	18
4th quintile	22	23	24
Richest quintile	47	42	38

Source: Calculations from Moldova Household Survey, Georgia Poverty Assessment (1999), World Bank data.

This pattern of the distribution of consumption has remained relatively unaffected by the onset of the regional crisis, which, while lowering absolute incomes, has generally preserved the distribution while improving it slightly in urban areas (Figure II). While the absolute level of consumption is still meager by international standards, it was ten times the average consumption of the poorest fifth of the population.

The report first investigates the state of poverty in Moldova. It then goes on, in turn, to look at the two issues outlined above: how the macro-labor environment can contribute to increased incomes as a way out of poverty, and how the Moldovan State can best help those left out of any growth process.

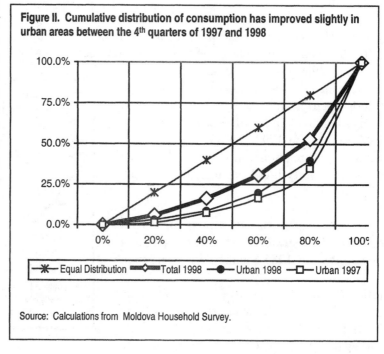

Figure II. Cumulative distribution of consumption has improved slightly in urban areas between the 4th quarters of 1997 and 1998

Equal Distribution — Total 1998 — Urban 1998 — Urban 1997

Source: Calculations from Moldova Household Survey.

---

1. WHO ARE THE POOR?

➢ *Poverty is more prevalent in rural areas than in other urban areas. Moreover, those who live in Chisinau are much better off than those in other cities.*
➢ *Low labor market outcomes are reflected in the finding that the poorest groups in Moldova are the working poor, especially the landless in agriculture.*
➢ *Some elderly people are poor, but pensioners may not be at special risk of poverty.*
➢ *Women are less poor than men, but the difference narrows with age.*

Those who live in urban areas are better off than their rural counterparts, both in terms of absolute and relative poverty. Those who live in Chisinau are especially well off. In August 1997, per capita consumption in rural areas was only 75 percent of that in urban areas—with the poorest 20 percent of the population in rural Moldova consuming about 73 percent of the corresponding consumption of the urban poor. Similarly, only 6.7 percent of the population in Chisinau were found to be relatively poor, compared to 17.2 percent of the population of other cities, and 21.1 percent of the rural population. The finding is at variance with the situation in some of the other former Soviet countries, where rural farmers were often better off because they could consume their own produce. A reason, however, why urban Moldovans are not at a disadvantage in terms of self-produced food may be the fairly widespread ownership of dacha plots in the countryside by urban Moldovans, the frequent travel to the countryside by urban dwellers (especially in summer) and the continuing close ties with family in rural areas.

Mirroring the geographical distribution described above, agricultural workers (as opposed to farmers) are occupationally the most vulnerable group in Moldova. In May 1997, 27 percent of agricultural workers were below the relative poverty line, as compared to just 15 percent of farmers, and 21 percent of the unemployed (Figure III). The slow progress in structural transformation in Moldovan agriculture is an explanation. Moldova, unlike the countries in the Caucasus, did not undergo land reform in the early years since independence. In 1997, most farms were still unreformed *kolkhozi* (collective farms) or *sovkhozi* (State farms). With Soviet input and output channels in disarray, and existing sales mostly in barter, the farms are chronically unable to pay wages to workers, especially in cash. The process of farm restructuring, underway today in Moldova, is rapidly changing this situation.

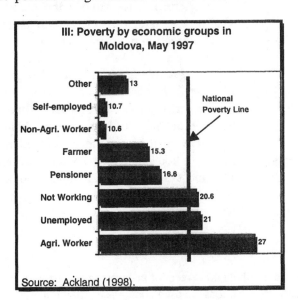

III: Poverty by economic groups in Moldova, May 1997

Source: Ackland (1998).

Families with children are among the poorest group in Moldova. Overall, data from August 1997 shows that almost 18 percent of all Moldovans were poor. But almost 30 percent of those in households with children, and without elderly members, were poor. Families with only children were also more likely to be poor than those with both children and elderly members (Table II). This may partly be because of the child care that an elderly grandparent is able to provide while the parents are engaged in agriculture, and partly because the elderly may have other sources of income from pensions or assets. (Figure IV).[3]

Although some of the elderly with particular vulnerabilities are poor, the older generation as a whole is not necessarily the poorest group in Moldova. The elderly, 17 percent of the population, are just 10.5 percent of the poor. Yet, this is in contradiction to popular opinion, and deserves some explanation. One possibility is that senior or more well-established families might have preferential access to more or better land and housing. Perhaps as importantly, many of the elderly were able to accumulate other physical assets during their working life in Soviet times. On the other hand, members of younger households, especially those entering the workforce in post-independence Moldova, have had fewer opportunities for well-paying jobs and asset accumulation.

Table II: The poor and family composition (poor as % of total)		
In households with:	Children	No Children
Elderly	23.7	17.0
No elderly	29.9	12.6

Source: Ackland (1998).

Figure IV. Who are the poor?

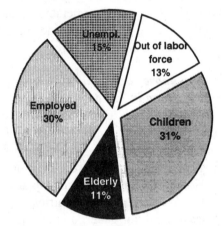

Source: Lindauer (1997).

But some sections of the elderly are, indeed, very poor. Those living alone, or depending exclusively on their pensions for support, may be extremely vulnerable. Those who are no longer capable of physically cultivating their land (including urban gardens) often lease their land to others, in exchange for what is sometimes a very meager portion of the harvest. Special efforts have to be made, therefore, to identify the elderly with these characteristics, and to target social protection payments to them.

Households with more than five members, or with more than two children, are likely to be poor. Almost 1.2 million people live in households with five or more members. Of them, over 400,000 (35 percent) are poor.[4] The numbers increase with household size, so that four out of ten people in households over seven members, and almost all of those in nine-member households, are poor.

---

[3] The poverty line used is a "relative" one, using as the threshold 40 percent of the average consumption. These results are, however, quite sensitive to what assumptions are used about the distribution of consumption within households. Here, it is assumed that an additional family member consumes as much as any other. If, on the other hand, additional family members consumed smaller marginal amounts (there were "economies of scale" in consumption), members of larger families could be considered to be less poor than in these findings.

[4] Once again, this calculation does involve assumptions about "economies of scale." If we assume that each additional household member does not consume as much as previous members, the poverty status of large households would be better than calculated here.

Even within these households, poverty depends on how many of the family members are children 14 and under. Almost one out of three of those living in families with two children are poor, and 42 percent of those in households with three or more children suffer from poverty. This is partly because of the family's "dependency burden"—the need to support non-earning members of a family on one or two incomes. Every 100 workers in Moldova support 167 dependents—children, the non-working elderly, the unemployed and those out of the labor force. (This compares, for example, to 114 dependents per 100 workers in the United States).

2. POVERTY AND RELATIVE PRICES

➢ *Relative price shocks, especially the steep rise in energy prices in recent years, has affected living standards in Moldova.*

➢ *But food-related poverty is lower, partly because low demand for agricultural exports has kept domestic consumer prices low. Given that food is the largest part of the consumption basket for the poor, this has been a key factor in moderating the growth in poverty in the recent past.*

The poverty of individuals and households in Moldova have mirrored the causes of the overall slowdown in the economy. Many enterprises found that the post-Soviet economic structure resulted in a vast increase in the ratio of their input prices to the market price of their output. Similarly, consumers found that the market prices of necessities—food and especially energy—were relatively (and in a few cases, absolutely) greater than the price their labor could fetch in the new recessionary labor market.

Table III: Consumption budget shares, May 1997 (poor as % of total)		
	Poor	All
Food and beverages	82.5	67.9
Rent, utilities	2.6	5.4
Clothing and footwear	2.3	4.9
Alcohol, tobacco	1.9	3.1
Health care	1.7	2.5
Housing—furnishings etc.	1.6	2.1
Transportation	1.0	2.0
Entertainment, eating out	0.8	0.9
Education	0.0	0.1
Other	0.7	1.6
Source: Ackland (1998).		

Yet Moldova, as an agricultural producer, has been able to protect its consumers reasonably well against increases in food prices—and thus food-related poverty is still relatively low. This has been especially true due to the economy-wide price stabilization since 1995, but has also been because of the large amount of self-production of food. In more recent years, and particularly in the latter half of 1998, food prices have also been driven down greatly by the loss of traditional export markets, especially Russia. As a result, there has been an excess supply of food to the domestic market (especially Chisinau), driving prices down greatly. Given the relative abundance of agricultural commodities, consumers were also able to switch fairly easily between products within food groups as the within-group relative prices changed—the switch by the poor away from bread to mamaliga being a good example. With food and beverages being four-fifths of the poor's consumption basket (Table III), the price effect on the poor's overall consumption has not been as great.

The largest change in relative prices faced by Moldova, and more recently by Moldovans, has been in energy costs. Moldova, which imports almost all of its energy in the form of gas and electricity from Russia and Ukraine respectively, had long enjoyed subsidized prices for the energy. It paid for energy imports with exports of agricultural and other goods. With the breakdown of Soviet trading practices, the price of energy has risen significantly. Between 1995 and 1997, the price of electricity to consumers rose by around 15 percent. Then, faced by a ruinous external debt due to energy non-payments and underpayments, the Government was forced, in June 1997, to initiate a series of major price increases. For electricity, household tariffs rose again by more than 20 percent. At the same time, household tariffs for gas rose by 40 percent. Most drastic was the increase in district heating tariffs, by about 90 percent over previous levels. In late 1998, the tariff for heating increased again, by a further 60 percent.

This has caused problems as centralized heating is now difficult for most households to afford, and the Government cannot afford to fully subsidize heating charges for the entire urban population. However, the poor do not spend very much on energy (in May 1997, 2.6 percent of the poor's consumption was on rents and utilities—see Table III). This is partly because there are no effective measures to ensure payment for heat, which is the component of energy for which prices have increased the most.[5]

---

3. POVERTY AND INCOMES

> *Moldovans who have jobs are only slightly less likely to be poor than those who are unemployed or on unpaid leave. Formal employment has become less secure, and young school-leavers and women with child care responsibilities find it difficult to find such employment.*
> *Food production in dacha plots has become a critical survival strategy for both the employed and unemployed. Informal sector activities, including labor migration, have provided necessary cash.*
> *To address this problem, the State should create an environment that allows enterprises to flourish, and thus demand labor at high wages.*
> *The farm restructuring process is a critical element in this direction, providing assets and the means to generate income to some of the poorest in Moldovan society.*
> *Only rapid growth would reduce absolute poverty over the medium term, with inequality-reducing, rural-based growth achieving the objective much more quickly.*

Official unemployment rates are very low, but greatly underestimate the true number of those out of work. Registered unemployment in Moldova is about 23,000 workers (roughly one percent of the adult population). But, if we include workers who are on forced or unpaid leaves from their enterprises (who, since they neither report to their workplace or receive a salary, are functionally unemployed), the official unemployment rate rises to over 12 percent of the labor force. But data from the household survey presents an even more serious picture—the rate of unemployment and unpaid leave is closer to 28 percent of the labor force (Figure V).

---

[5] Although the share may have increased since May 1997, the overall effect of prices on consumption is still likely to be overwhelmingly dominated by food-related expenses.

The majority of the unemployed in Moldova do not register as unemployed, because the costs of doing so outweigh the benefits. The benefits include eligibility to receive modest unemployment benefits, and access to training and job placement services. For those on forced or unpaid leave, the costs of registering as unemployed include forsaking any enterprise-related benefits, especially housing or medical services, that they may be receiving. From the perspective of an enterprise, if workers are permanently laid-off, the firm is legally obliged to make severance payments. This provision creates a disincentive to officially fire workers.

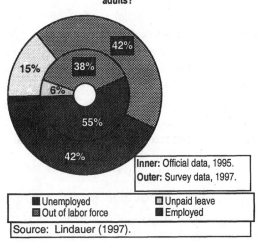

Figure V. What is the employment status of adults?

Inner: Official data, 1995.
Outer: Survey data, 1997.

■ Unemployed   ▨ Unpaid leave
▨ Out of labor force   ▨ Employed

Source: Lindauer (1997).

Being officially employed or not has a very small effect of whether a person is poor. Although the poverty rate (the chance that someone is poor) for the unemployed is higher than for the employed, the difference is not large. Those with jobs have about a 22 percent chance of being poor, while the unemployed have about a 28 percent chance of being poor. This similarity is due primarily to two reasons. Those who are employed often receive extremely low compensation (January 1997 wages were 190 lei per month, or about US$500 per year, in enterprises with more than 20 employees). To make matters worse, salary payments in many enterprises, especially those in agriculture and heavy industry, are often delayed by several months. On the other hand, the officially unemployed rarely depend on the State's unemployment benefits to survive. Relying on trade, seasonal employment, and transfers from family members, many of them are somehow able to make ends meet.

Subsistence or garden agriculture is a key source of income for most Moldovan households. In addition, petty trade and small home-based enterprises have become an important support. Most of the poor try to combine several strategies at once: some formal employment, subsistence agriculture, and part- or full-time trading or production. For rural, small-town, and even some urban residents, subsistence farming has become the mainstay of household economies. This may be on the nominally restructured collective farms, on privatized "peasant farms", or on household or dacha plots (for which over a million rural households now have title). The dacha plots also provide food to supplement their own consumption. Rural households also supplement their income from collective farms by private husbandry—raising turkeys, chickens, cows and pigs for sale in the market or to individual exporters. In cities and towns, private vehicles are used to provide informal taxi services, and rooms are rented. Foreign trips of short duration are taken to buy goods for resale in local markets. Finally, as circumstances become more strained, bribery, extortion, prostitution, theft and other forms of criminal activity are increasingly resorted to as a means of securing income.

As in other former Soviet countries, labor migration has become the quickest and often riskiest way to earn cash. Unable to find productive income-earning opportunities in Moldova, the more enterprising and able-bodied Moldovans are leaving the country to seek employment as guest workers, and are sending much of their earnings back as remittances. Migrants go to Russia, Ukraine and Belarus (as construction or agricultural workers), Hungary and Romania (for trade), Greece (for agricultural work, housework, and child care), Turkey (to market produce), Germany, Israel and elsewhere. Most often, such migration is not legal, and involves considerable hazards, both from the authorities and from informal extortionists and criminals. In 1996, only 11,000 Moldovan nationals were officially registered as working abroad (the majority in Russia). Nevertheless, informal estimates put the true figure at perhaps 15 times that amount, including those who are unregistered temporary migrants traveling in search of employment.

Creation of productive employment opportunities is crucial to poverty alleviation. But this does not imply that the Government should go back to creating employment or sustaining jobs in state enterprises which are not commercially viable. When low unemployment is the result of maintaining large numbers of workers in unproductive jobs, social welfare is compromised. This is because such a policy, in the long run, results in either wage arrears or the need for large transfers from the budget. Such transfers may contribute to inflation—and inflation hurts the poor the most. Instead, the Government has to create conditions for economic growth that, in turn, creates the demand for labor—where it will be in the enterprises' own interests to hire more workers at higher wages.

The recent reforms in agriculture are a promising step in this direction. Farm restructuring in agriculture, which is breaking up large and unviable *kolkhozi* and *sovkhozi*, is expected to be completed by the end of 2000. This is creating a new class of private farmers with titles to their land, and allowing them to either farm the land themselves or lease it out to obtain income. As has been seen in Figure III, private farmers are significantly less poor than agricultural workers, who suffer from low and late wages. Preliminary indications are that the

---

TOOL BOX I: Growth simulations

Only rapid growth in consumption will yield a large improvement in the welfare of the poor over the short run. What patterns of growth would yield the best results for Moldova? The answer is clearly growth that favors rural areas, and growth that improves inequality.

We consider two illustrative scenarios: a case of balanced growth, and inequality-reducing growth. It should be noted that the simulations are not intended to be forecasts, but examples to demonstrate the effects of different growth patterns for Moldova. First, consider the scenario where everyone's consumption increases across the board at the optimistic average growth rate of 5 percent a year. In this stylized case, the absolute poverty headcount (the number of people consuming below the equivalent of 82.10 lei in May 1997) would fall from 46 percent in 1998 to 27.7 percent by 2004. The poverty headcount will drop to below 20 percent by the year 2008. If average growth rates are slower, the reduction of poverty to below 20 percent will take longer.

But, for such balanced growth, rural poverty (53.6 percent in 1998) would remain consistently higher than poverty in urban areas (33.2 percent in 1998). And the distribution of incomes will actually get worse, as the income disparity between rich and poor widens.

Agriculture-driven growth, however, has a chance of reversing this situation. Consider if this growth was driven by rising consumption in rural areas than urban (say, an average consumption growth of 6.5 percent in rural areas, versus 3 percent in urban, still giving us about 5 percent growth overall). Then, while overall rates of poverty reduction would be similar, rural poverty would decline faster, to drop below urban poverty rates (19 percent compared to 20.4 percent) by 2007.

Finally, what pattern of growth would improve Moldova's levels of inequality to those in Western European countries (i.e., around 0.3 as opposed to over 0.4 today)? Again, using the benchmark overall growth rate of 5 percent a year, this would happen within ten years if the consumption of the poorest grew much faster than those of the richest. In a simulation where the consumption of the poorest 40 percent grows at three times the rate of growth of the richest 20 percent, the Gini falls to 0.3 by 2009, comparable to the levels of inequality in France or Germany today. Most strikingly, such inequality-reducing growth patterns also reduces poverty much faster compared to the other situations.

---

transfer of income generating assets to the workers has, indeed, resulted in increased incomes for the beneficiaries, and may be the way towards reducing rural poverty in Moldova. This would also reduce overall poverty in Moldova faster, and, by increasing incomes and consumption for rural laborers, among the poorest in Moldova, may be inequality-reducing (Tool Box I).

4. SOCIAL PROTECTION STRATEGIES

➤ *The capability of Moldova's Government to provide for social protection has been compromised by its fiscal crisis, and marked by expenditure arrears.*

➤ *The social assistance system is rudimentary, and relies heavily on pensions and an array of untargeted and unfunded privileges to those deemed worthy rather than needy.*

➤ *The Government is reinventing the system of privileges, taking steps to eliminate them for the less needy and replacing them, over the medium term, with a transfer targeted to the needy.*

➤ *Over the medium term, as resources become available, "self-targeted" programs will need to be developed and utilized, and the Government will have to move towards a targeted cash transfer mechanism.*

The Government has been increasingly unable to meet its expenditure commitments, and the result has been a run-up of arrears. Public sector expenditure arrears, to public employees, pensioners and suppliers (especially suppliers of energy) have been mounting steadily since the mid-1990s, to reach 11.4 percent of GDP in end-1998, almost half of actual tax collections for the year. Over the past half-decade, the situation has worsened, due to a continued combination of overstated revenue targets, lack of provision for anticipated expenditure shocks and a lack of monitoring and control over local government spending, which have all essentially conspired to create a situation of "planned arrears".

The social protection system is mostly unreformed from its historical design. In Soviet times, all people of working age worked, and older people received pension payments. Although formal wage payments were low, there were significant non-wage benefits, as well as price controls and subsidies on consumer goods. Therefore, only those totally cut off from the formal labor market were considered to be in need of special interventions. Poverty was regarded as a social pathology, and these "excess" cases included alcoholics, the handicapped, vagrants or the elderly infirm. The Moldovan social protection system is still oriented towards this old philosophy.

Moldova, like many FSU countries, has a broad array of special privileges for specific categories of people deemed to be 'worthy', not necessarily needy. Overall, almost 1.3 million Moldovans (well over a third of the population) enjoy these privileges, which depending on the beneficiary, can be benefiting either the poorer sections of society or the non-poor. The key, however, is that few of them were instituted as pro-poor measures—instead, they were rewards given to certain "worthy" sections of the population that the Soviet society wanted to recognize and subsidize.

The system is extremely expensive for the economy as a whole, and particularly for the enterprise (mostly in the energy and transport sectors) supplying the privilege. Privileges are essentially an implicit subsidy provided by an enterprise. Technically, the Government is supposed to compensate the enterprise for this subsidy. The mechanism for this compensation is, however, complex, and the Government has in recent years simply not budgeted enough to pay for the privileges. In 1998, privileges cost the economy over 800 million lei (around 8 percent of GDP).

Table IV: Share of Government transfers received (% of total)		
Households:	Poor	Non-Poor
Sickness/maternity benefit	0	100
Social pension	0	100
Early retirement pension	15	85
Old age pension	17	83
Student stipend	16	84
Disability pension	20	80
Elderly care benefit	20	80
Child allowances	32	68
Unemployment benefit	65	35

Source: Braithwaite (1997).

The Government, in 1999, has begun taking actions to rationalize its privileges and compensation strategy. The Government has a four-tiered strategy in this area: (a) remove the communal services compensation scheme, which is poorly targeted, and unaffordable for the budget; (b) eliminate all energy and transportation privileges; (c) install in its place an interim energy compensation scheme targeted to specific categories of the population which are deemed to be most in need of social assistance, and ensure that payments are made in full and in cash to the beneficiaries; and (d) develop a comprehensive social assistance strategy for the medium to long term which eliminates all privileges, while putting in place an effectively targeted social assistance program that is tied in magnitude to the envelope of budget revenues in any given year.

In spite of the best intentions of policy-makers and individual social workers, the pension and social assistance systems are inequitable. More non-poor than poor households receive all sorts of government benefits, for every category except unemployment benefits. For maternity and sickness pay and social pensions, *all* the benefits "leak" to the non-poor (Table IV). Overall, as shown by Figure VI, although most of the poorest in society are covered by social assistance transfers, the bulk of the transfers themselves go to the better-off in society.

The system is also inefficient. Most pensioners (especially those in rural areas) receive pensions anywhere from a few weeks to nine months late. Moreover, distribution and access to assistance differs a great deal between city and village. The ethnographic survey found that, in November 1996, pensioners in Balti received their pension with delays of one or two weeks, while in nearby villages, pensions had not been received in 10 months.

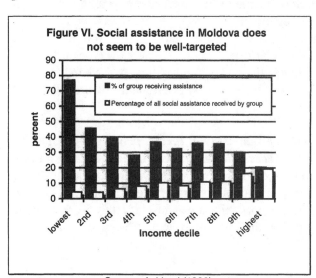

Figure VI. Social assistance in Moldova does not seem to be well-targeted

- % of group receiving assistance
- Percentage of all social assistance received by group

Source: Ackland (1998).

Any reform in the system of social assistance in Moldova has to be built on increased access to the poor, and cost-effectiveness. The reform will have to acknowledge that the traditional groups receiving social assistance (including privileges) may only comprise a small part of those most in need—and many of these groups may be less vulnerable, and thus less in need of protection, than others. Since current resources are very restricted, they should be narrowly spent to bring about the greatest improvements in the living standards for the poorest. As the resources of the Government increase, the social assistance mechanism could also expand, so that the Government is able to help provide a better standard of living to more of the population. However, creating an entitlement system by, for example, legislating that all individuals are entitled to a certain percentage of an arbitrarily determined "minimum existence level" could prove to be disastrous, since the resulting transfer system would have no link to the resources actually available to the Government. The broad principles for this realignment of social protection are given in Policy Box I.

POLICY BOX I: Principles to guide Moldova's social protection philosophy

➤ The generation of sufficient fiscal resources through the elimination or drastic reduction of transfers that are either wasteful or badly targeted to the poor. This includes privileges, and some categories of social assistance benefits. This needs to be accompanied by an examination of the existing system of social protection, in order to clearly determine the rationale and utility of each of the multitude of overlapping benefits.

➤ As resources (or donor funds) permit, the creation of "self-targeted" assistance programs to help the poor (especially in rural areas) weather sudden economic shocks.

➤ *Over the medium term, a move towards the creation of a comprehensive targeting mechanism* that would allow an expansion of the social safety net to cover more people as the Government's resources expand.

---

5. STRATEGIES FOR SOCIAL SECTOR EXPENDITURES

➤ *In health and education, public expenditures have been falling and major structural reforms have not occurred.*

➤ *This has left a system that provides inadequate services to most, and is mostly unaffordable to the poor.*

➤ *Access to health care needs significant informal payments for services and supplies, and educational access is falling mostly due to the declining demand caused by the inability of the poorest families to afford the ancillary costs of education, especially in rural areas.*

➤ *Lack of access to education is particularly worrisome, given high rates of returns to literacy, and to higher education.*

➤ *The systems will have to be structurally changed, to reduce the overall inefficiency and ensure the availability of basic services to the poor. This may entail a focus on primary over tertiary care in both health and education, and a more efficient and effective funding of education and health services in rural areas.*

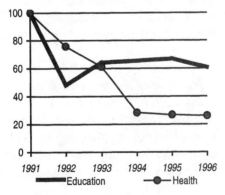

Figure VII: Real public social sector spending has decreased

Figures include both left and right banks (1991=100).
Source: Calculated from World Bank data.

Reduced budgetary expenditures and the inability of the education and health systems in Moldova to adjust to the new realities of transition has meant that the human capital of the poor is worsening. Both education and health care in Moldova, especially at the basic levels, is provided by the Government. Budget allocations to these two sectors, however, are meager and decreasing (Figure VII)—9.4 percent of GDP for education and just 6.4 percent of GDP for health in 1996.

To compound the problem, these funds are spent inefficiently, with a large proportion going to the tertiary level and a lack of cost recovery even from those who can afford it. At the same time, health workers and teachers are grossly underpaid (annual salaries range from the equivalent of US$330-600 for doctors and an average of US$430 for teachers), and often have several months' lag in wage payments. They now informally charge for their services, in cash or in the form of "gifts", creating a de facto system of private medicine and education. The poor are the worst off in this process, being unable to afford these informal fees.

The health care status of Moldovans is worsening, with the poor suffering the most. The crude death rate (death rate per 1,000 persons) increased markedly from 9.7 in 1990 to 11.5 in 1996, and the infant mortality rate increased from 19.0 per 1,000 live births in 1990 to 20.2 in 1996. The incidence of diseases such as tuberculosis, hepatitis, circulatory diseases, malignant neoplasms and syphilis have also increased rapidly since independence. Overall, poor families are visiting primary health care services almost 40 percent less often than the non-poor, although their use of hospital services are on par. The poor's expenditures on health care was just over 7.5 percent of their non-food expenditures, and only 12 percent of the corresponding expenditures by the non-poor. Illnesses needing hospital care are particularly unaffordable, since patients must provide everything from bed linens to syringes. For the poor, therefore, ill health bears a double burden—if untreated, it threatens their ability to keep their jobs, and if treated, it drains limited resources.

> **POLICY BOX II: Pillars of health care reform in Moldova**
>
> ➢ *Restructuring the over-sized provider network*, to release resources from tertiary-level health care to primary level care.
> ➢ *Strengthening the primary care network*, through increased resources funding the establishment of an effective network of general practitioners.
> ➢ *Formalizing the existing informal payments*, to protect payments from arbitrary and excessive health care costs that are especially burdensome for the poor.
> ➢ *Redefining the basic health care package in line with budgetary resources*, with the majority of resources going towards primary care.
> ➢ *Centralized funding of health care* to improve the intra-sectoral allocation of resources.
> ➢ *Organizational reforms to make health service providers financial and managerially autonomous entities* without direct budgetary support.

The health care system needs a comprehensive overhaul, marked by a reduction in excess capacity, and a realignment of the resources released by this to strengthening the primary care network and safeguarding basic public health. Currently, too much of health expenditures, low as they are, are spent on hospitals—which do not always serve the basic needs of the poor. A realignment of services, focusing on primary care, would orient the system more towards the poor, while improving overall efficiency (and, over the medium run, providing enough resources to reduce the out-of-pocket expenditures by the poor to obtain health services) (Policy Box II).

The falling demand for education is due to falling quality and rising cost, and once again, the poorest are the worst affected. The access of poor children and youth to good education is being reduced by a combination of factors. These include the deterioration of infrastructure, the outflow of qualified teachers, the cost of school supplies and even the lack of adequate clothing in winter. With the inability of the state to adequately fund education, private schools, tutors, and private institutions of higher education have moved in. But the quality of the education offered by them varies, and they are unaffordable for the poor.

Additionally, absenteeism among poor children is becoming endemic, as they drop out to join the labor force, primarily in subsistence or wage agriculture. Overall, over 15 percent of poor children were not going to school in 1997, with the problem being worse for girls in rural areas. In higher education, only 14 percent of poor Moldovans between 17 and 24 of age were enrolled, compared to 40 percent of the youth from non-poor households. This difference in educational access threatens to have serious consequences for the future—with the children of the poor also doomed to remain poor because of their relative lack of education and skills.

This is especially worrisome given the high returns to education that are seen in Moldova. There is a monotonically increasing relationship between incidence of poverty and lower educational attainment of individuals aged 14 years and over. The difference that education makes is marked. In May 1997, the poverty rate for a person with higher education was 7.3 percent compared with 25.8 percent for an illiterate person. There is a risk, therefore, that poor educational access by today's poor children may drag them into poverty as adults.

In education, restructuring will have to be done over the longer run, with a focus on reallocating public resources from tertiary education to primary and secondary schools, especially in rural areas. Income growth and its distribution will also be the key influences in the long-run. Greater cost recovery for higher education, and for optional courses (such as music and languages) at lower education levels, will also release resources that can be best targeted to the poor. Over the longer time horizon, however, increased incomes, by lowering the opportunity costs to poor households of sending their children to school, will allow them to focus on investing in education rather than on just how to meet consumption needs.

6. AN ANTI-POVERTY STRATEGY FOR MOLDOVA

Much of poverty in Moldova is a labor market phenomenon, driven by the reduced opportunities for remunerative work in the economy. The high incidence of poverty among the working poor, especially agricultural workers, on the one hand (which demonstrates the low wage levels in stagnant occupations), and the high poverty among the unemployed and those on unpaid leave on the other (which points to the lack of good jobs) drive much of the poverty in the nation. Therefore, the fundamental approach to reducing poverty in Moldova will have to be through increasing growth and income opportunities for the population, particularly in rural areas.

At the same time, poverty is also high among those outside the workforce, including the disabled and a part of the more vulnerable among the elderly. Thus, in addition, efforts will have to be made to find ways to reach them, through both private and public means. However, this is going to be constrained by limited public resources, which in turn is connected to the decline in the economy.

Access to human capital, because it affects the ability of people to obtain and retain remunerative work, is a critical element of any anti-poverty strategy. The low rates of access to education by the poor that are found in Moldova would imply the creation of an inter-generational cycle of poverty, as the poor children of today do not get access to better-earning jobs in the future. Similarly, lack of access to primary health services jeopardizes the ability of the poor to work for a living.

Moldova's poverty alleviation strategy therefore has to rest on two pillars:

➤ Sustained economic growth that generates productive employment and thus higher wages, with a focus on rural-centered growth that reduces inequalities and empowers people to increase their own earnings abilities; and

➤ A focus on improving the poor's access to social services and a safety net, underpinned by improved efficiency of the public sector revenue generation and expenditure management.

The first pillar, therefore, deals with key elements needed to increase the ability of individuals to lift themselves out of poverty. This will happen as the Moldovan labor market begins to create more employment at higher wages. A resumption of economic growth is, of course, the cornerstone. This economic growth will have to flow from increased investment, diversified trade, a conducive macro environment and restructuring of enterprises (especially agricultural collective farms, which are the primary source of employment in Moldova). This agriculture-based growth will also help reduce inequality, by improving the ability of the working poor, who are primarily in rural areas, to improve their earnings. As discussed, the preservation of human capital through access to health and education (a part of the second pillar, below) will also play a key role in this revival.

The second pillar concerns the options and constraints for the Government to provide a helping hand to those unable to get out of poverty. The most prominent instruments of direct intervention by the Government are its social assistance and insurance programs. These, however, need to be adequately funded and thus need fiscal resources—and therefore may need to be considered only in the medium term. The resumption of growth, a part of the first pillar, is a necessary condition for this second pillar, as it will allow greater fiscal resources. Resources will also be obtained as the economy sheds itself of untargeted privileges and other transfers, and redirects public spending on social sectors to the most needy. Across-the-board poverty reduction in Moldova will require both pillars of this strategy—each, without the other, is incomplete and would not be sustainable.

Moldova's Government, therefore, faces a critical challenge—how to protect the population today while laying the foundations for a better tomorrow. It will only be able to achieve this if it can take bold and far-sighted reforms that stop the wastage of scarce financial resources, provide the current generation with social support that is equitable and fair, and transform the macroeconomic environment to one that supports increased incomes for all (Policy Box III).

POLICY BOX III: Elements of an anti-poverty strategy for Moldova

The elements of a comprehensive medium-term poverty reduction strategy for Moldova would have the following elements:

1. *FIRST PILLAR: Sustained, inequality-reducing economic growth that generates productive employment and thus higher wages for workers.*

    ➢ **Restructuring in the agricultural sector** would be the first step towards this objective, accompanied by appropriate extension services. This would allow the poorest landless workers in rural areas to increase their ability to earn a living.

    ➢ The increased involvement of **foreign investors in agro-processing industries** will help to promote industrial recovery, and provide a source of demand for the produce of the agricultural sector.

    ➢ This needs to be accompanied by the removal of implicit and explicit barriers to **growth of small and medium enterprises**, in order to again lower the inequality of income opportunities for the poor versus the rich in the economy.

2. *SECOND PILLAR: Improving the poor's access to social services and a safety net, underpinned by improved efficiency of the public sector revenue generation and expenditure management.*

    ➢ Improved revenue generation, through a broadening of the tax base and more effective collection. Government expenditures streamlined to be the most efficient, while keeping a clear focus on the impact of expenditures on the poorest in society.

    ➢ **Social protection** transfers and mechanisms should be streamlined to channel the limited resources to just the poorest in society. Privileges would be removed from those deemed worthy, and given only to those who are seen to be needy. Over time, as resources permit, replacing the array of social benefits with targeted cash transfers, and self-targeted programs.

    ➢ **Ensuring access to basic social services** by the poorest in society, embedded in broader reforms for the social sectors. Over the medium term, health care reform would restructure the provision system to eliminate excess capacity at the tertiary level and focus on the provision of primary care and public health that is most needed by the poor, with an increased emphasis on rural health care facilities. Moreover, public funding for education would redistribute resources to primary and secondary education, to ensure that out-of-pocket costs of accessing education by the poor are reduced.

1. POVERTY AND TRANSITION

Moldova has suffered one of the steepest falls in incomes in the former Soviet Union, to the extent that it is likely to remain a low-income country for the near future. The fall in incomes has been caused by a prolonged recession as the economy struggles to reinvent itself in the market context, in an environment beset by external shocks. The new class of Moldova's poor, therefore, are mostly those for whom the transition has been difficult. They include younger families, who have struggled to mesh their existing skills with the narrowly-focused demands of the new marketplace. The poor are also overwhelmingly rural, especially agricultural wage workers—a legacy of the slower process of agricultural transformation until 1997. The elderly are also at risk, although not as much as popular perception would have it. Educational attainment also makes a significant difference—those with higher education are seldom poor, while the illiterate are more likely to be poor than the average.

INTRODUCTION: POLICY CHOICES ON POVERTY

In years ahead, the polity and society in Moldova have to come to terms with four facts, and design policy accordingly:

Moldova is no longer a middle-income nation. In terms of their *average* income and expenditures, Moldovans are at the level of their compatriots in countries that have a long history of poverty. This, on the one hand, means that a section of the population is in absolute poverty. On the other hand, though inequality is not extremely high by international standards, *relative* poverty is also an issue, with almost one-fifth of the population consuming less than 40 percent of average consumption. Government policymakers have to take this explicitly into account when designing policy, so that expectations generated by Moldova's middle-income past do not undermine a focus on the best solution to today's problems.

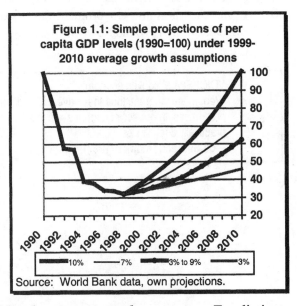

Figure 1.1: Simple projections of per capita GDP levels (1990=100) under 1999-2010 average growth assumptions

Source: World Bank data, own projections.

Poverty in Moldova cannot be considered a temporary phenomenon. To eliminate poverty over the medium term, the only solution is employment-generating growth. But even rapid and sustained growth, such as that experienced by countries in the Caucasus in the mid-1990s, is unlikely to bring Moldova back to previous levels of living standards. As an instance, consider the illustrative scenarios in Figure 1.1: it would require an average growth rate of the economy of 10 per cent per annum until the year 2010 to raise per capita GDP to the 1990 level.

A more probable, but still optimistic, scenario of gradually increasing growth rates until the year 2010[1] only takes per capita GDP to just over two-third of the 1990 level.

While economic growth is the only solution to alleviating poverty in general, it will not be sufficient to eradicate poverty. Rapid economic growth, even if it occurs, is not likely to eradicate the inequality that is present in today's Moldova. Once again, an illustration: with inequality patterns remaining the same, even the hypothetical 10 percent a year growth path described above would imply that the poorest one-fifth of the population lives on less than US$ 100 a month in 2009 (measured in 1997 dollars). With the gradually increasing growth rate path, their monthly incomes would be below US$60. Therefore, the Government does have a clear, if limited, role in protecting the poorest in society—those who would be left out by economic growth.

The Government has limited resources, and limited ability, to protect a large majority of the population. The unfortunate consequence of Moldova's prolonged recession is that almost all parts of the population are experiencing some level of deprivation. Therefore, the Government has to concentrate its efforts in three areas: (a) fostering an environment that allows individuals and families to increase their own incomes; (b) targeting its limited social protection resources only to those families who are the poorest in society (perhaps through a mechanism that allows the Government to increase its safety net to cover more people if its resources increase); and (c) looking to the future, and ensuring that the poor have adequate access to essential education and health services.

The remainder of this chapter focuses on the dimensions of poverty—on who and where the poor are in Moldova. The next two chapters lay out a blueprint for addressing the problems. First, what the Government can do to help those of the poor able to help themselves out of poverty, and then how the Government can focus its scarce resources to best assist those who find it difficult to improve their own welfare even when there is overall economic growth.

VOICES: A Moldovan economist
"People are different, thus they have to live differently. This gap exists, but it should not exist in such proportions. In our society, there are a few rich people but more and more poor ones; a middle class practically doesn't exist."
—de Soto and Dudwick (1997)

---

[1] This simulation assumes no growth in 1999, followed by 3 percent growth in 2000-01, 5 percent in 2002-03, and then increasing in two-year steps to 9 percent in 2009.

INTRODUCTION: THE BACKDROP TO POLICY CHOICES ON POVERTY

Today, Moldova is one of the poorest countries in Europe. Moldova had a per capita income of about $540 in 1997, in sharp contrast to the situation soon after its independence.[2,3] In 1992, estimates of Moldova's per capita GDP, in purchasing power parity terms, was about $3,700. Thus, the average Moldovan was, at the time, substantially richer than his or her

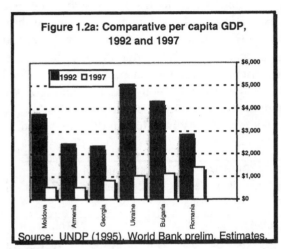

Figure 1.2a: Comparative per capita GDP, 1992 and 1997

Source: UNDP (1995). World Bank prelim. Estimates.

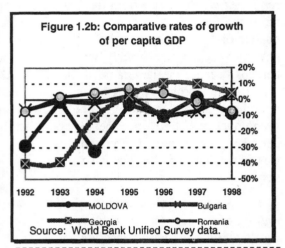

Figure 1.2b: Comparative rates of growth of per capita GDP

Source: World Bank Unified Survey data.

counterpart in Armenia, Georgia, Romania, and Albania—though poorer than Ukrainians and Bulgarians (Figure 1.2a). But the transition experience during the 1990s varied greatly from one country to the other, and the Moldovan experience was particularly disappointing (Figure 1.2b). The fall in the rate of growth, for instance, was the largest of any of its neighbors with the exception of Georgia and Armenia. Unlike these countries in the Caucasus, the Moldovan economy never rebounded strongly to make up some of the losses. By 1997, real GDP in Moldova was about 38 percent of its GDP in 1990, one of the largest such drops for any country in Europe.

The drop was compounded in 1998, when Moldova was the country hit the hardest by the regional crisis. GDP fell by a further 8.6 percent in 1998. While almost every societal group felt the income shock, the worst affected

✓ **INDICATOR BOX 1.1a: Absolute poverty, if compared quarter to quarter, was greater in 1998 than in 1997**

Poverty Using Food Poverty Line (65.2 lei per month, May 97, adjusted for food price inflation)				
	1997 Q3	1997 Q4	1998 Q3	1998 Q4
P0	16.8%	24.2%	26.5%	25.3%
P1	5.2%	7.7%	8.6%	7.8%
P2	2.5%	3.7%	4.1%	3.5%

Poverty Using Absolute Poverty Line (82.1 lei per month, May 97, adjusted for inflation)				
	1997 Q3	1997 Q4	1998 Q3	1998 Q4
P0	30.4%	37.0%	41.3%	46.1%
P1	9.7%	13.2%	15.4%	15.8%
P2	4.7%	6.6%	7.8%	7.5%

Note: P0 is the "headcount" for poverty—the percentage of households with consumption below the poverty line; P1 is a measure of the "poverty gap" or depth of poverty, and P2 of the severity of poverty.
Source: Own calculations from Moldova Household Survey.

---

[2] These preliminary estimates for 1997 use the World Bank's "Synthetic Atlas" exchange rate, which is a proxy for the PPP (purchasing power parity) market exchange rate. Using market exchange rates, GNP per capita for Moldova is estimated to be $430.

[3] Unless explicitly mentioned otherwise, "Moldova" refers to the "Right Bank" of the Nistru river—that is, the numbers exclude the region of Transnistria., for which available data is meager and often unreliable.

were the poorest in society. Agricultural exports to Russia, the mainstay of the economy, fell in the latter half of 1998 due to weak demand and payments problems. The small domestic market became saturated with local produce, causing a sharp fall in output prices and rural cash incomes. At the same time, the fiscal crisis induced by the shock caused sharply increased arrears in wages and pension payments, further lowering the purchasing power of wage earners and vulnerable pensioners.

Absolute poverty increased as well due to the crisis, although relative poverty remained stable. Data from the last quarter of 1998 shows that food poverty (the value of a minimum food consumption bundle of 2100 calories a day) worsened significantly in the third quarter of 1998 compared to the third quarter of 1997 (Indicator Box 1.1a). However, food poverty was not significantly worse in the fourth quarter of 1998, after the regional crisis, perhaps because the large amount of unexported agricultural production caused a fall in food prices. An absolute poverty line (which adds on the value of non-food spending for the households at the food poverty line) shows a significant worsening of poverty in 1998. In the fourth quarter of 1998, more people consumed below this poverty line than in the corresponding period a year before. The poverty gap was wider, and poverty was also more severe.

Since independence, the welfare of the population has worsened significantly, in both absolute and relative terms. The 1997 Household Budget Survey found that the average Moldovan's consumption was just about 1,725 lei ($370) a year. But this consumption is heavily skewed by that of the relatively wealthier groups in the population—the richest 20 percent consumed about 4,300 lei ($925) a year. While this is still meager by international standards, it was ten times the average consumption of the poorest fifth of the population. The disparity is especially marked in the urban areas, where the richest quintile consume well over three-fifths of all consumption (Indicator Box 1.1b). Between 1997 and 1998, however, the distribution of income improved marginally, especially in urban areas (Figure 1.3).

The Gini index for consumption, a measure of inequality, therefore, was about

✓ **INDICATOR BOX 1.1b: The distribution of consumption improved slightly between end-1997 and end-1998**

(% of total)	URBAN		TOTAL	
	Q4 1997	Q4 1998	Q4 1997	Q4 1998
Poorest quintile	1.5	3.1	5.3	6.0
2nd quintile	5.9	5.6	9.9	10.3
3rd quintile	9.1	11.2	14.6	14.5
4th quintile	18.5	19.9	21.6	22.2
Richest quintile	65.0	60.3	48.6	47.0

Source: Calculations from Moldova Household Survey.

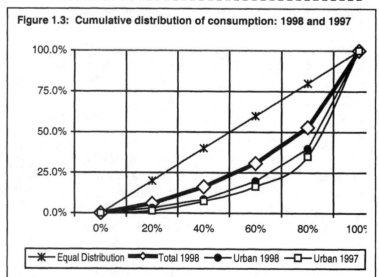

Figure 1.3: Cumulative distribution of consumption: 1998 and 1997

Source: Calculations from Moldova Household Survey.

40 for Moldova.[4] This is not uncommonly high for poor countries, or for countries in transition (Comparator Box 1.2). But the presence of such high inequality is still remarkable for a country and society that, during the last half century, had strived to achieve the goal of relative egalitarianism. Increasing inequality has produced significant stress in the social, economic and political fabric of Moldova. The history of the relatively well-off past in Moldova has collided with present day reality.

★ **COMPARATOR BOX 1.2: Moldova's level of inequality is similar to those in other transition countries**

Country	Year	Gini	GNP per capita
Vietnam	1993	35.7	170
Moldova	**1997**	**40.0**	**540**
China	1995	41.5	620
Romania	1992	25.5	1,130
Bulgaria	1992	30.8	1,330
Ukraine	1992	25.7	1,820
Poland	1992	27.2	1,910
Russia	1993	39.0	2,510
All transition	*1993-95*	*33.0*	--

Source: World Bank (1992, 1993, 1997), Milanovic (1998), own calculations.

WHO ARE THE POOR?

EMPLOYMENT, AGE AND GENDER DIMENSIONS OF POVERTY

The poor in Moldova today include both people who were traditionally economically vulnerable and those who enjoyed privileged lifestyles in Soviet times. The poor range from less educated, unskilled workers, or very large single-parent families, to highly educated persons who once enjoyed socially prestigious and well compensated positions as scientists and professionals.

Overall, about one in five Moldovans can be considered to be "relatively" poor. This is by using a measure that identifies the "poor" as those people whose consumption is below 40 percent of the average (Tool Box 1.10, at the end of the chapter, explains the rationale for this choice). This is comparable to similar "relative" poverty measures (Comparator Box 1.4) for other transition countries.

★ **COMPARATOR BOX 1.4: Moldova falls somewhere in the middle among transition countries in terms of its relative poverty**

Country	Poverty headcount 1993-95 (%)	GNP per capita (US$), 1994*
Moldova*	**24**	**540**
Kyrgyz Rep.	55	610
Romania	48	1,270
Ukraine	26	1,570
Belarus	14	2,160
Poland	10	2,410
Russia	39	2,650
Estonia	34	2,820
Hungary	7	3,840

Note: Moldova GNP per capita figures, for 1997. Different US$ poverty lines used for different countries, 1993-95.
Source: Calculations from the February 1997 Household Budget Survey, Milanovic (1998), Kuddo (1998).

---

[4] The Gini is an index of inequality that varies between zero and 100, with zero representing perfect equality and 100 perfect inequality.

Clearly, this is not a measure of absolute deprivation, and this measure is very sensitive to the choice of the base line. Therefore, headcounts for several other poverty lines are shown in Indicator Box 1.3.[5]

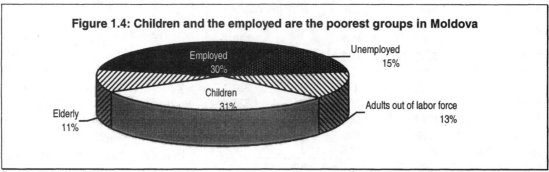

Figure 1.4: Children and the employed are the poorest groups in Moldova

Employed 30%
Unemployed 15%
Children 31%
Adults out of labor force 13%
Elderly 11%

Source: Lindauer (1998).

On the other hand, few Moldovans suffer from extreme poverty, as defined by the World Bank's Absolute Minimum Poverty Line of $1 per person per day. Yet, most Moldovans have a much lower absolute standard of living compared to Soviet days. For example, using the

✓ **INDICATOR BOX 1.3: 1997 poverty lines for Moldova are very different, depending on the standard chosen**

	February 1997		August 1997	
	Poverty line (lei)	Head-count	Poverty line (lei)	Head-count
Main (or 'base') poverty line : 40% of weighted per capita consumption	57.4	19.0%	63.65	17.9%
Alternative poverty lines:				
Sarkisiyan Minimum Consumption Basket (MCB)	415.00	96.9%	415.00	95.3%
Sarkisiyan MCB food portion	201.00	78.7%	201.00	77.4%
120% of base line	80.54	33.1%	76.38	26.2%
110% of base line	73.83	28.1%	70.01	21.3%
90% of base line	60.40	19.3%	57.28	14.4%
80% of base line	53.69	14.5%	50.92	11.4%
OECD per equivalent consumption [1/]	67.12	11.8%	63.65	8.9%
Absolute minimum PPP per capita poverty Line [2/]	14.40	0.9%	14.77	0.7%

Notes: Poverty lines are expressed in Moldovan lei per person per month. Headcounts are the weighted percentage of individuals with monthly expenditures below the relevant poverty line.
[1/] The OECD equivalence scale is as follows: first adult in household = 1.0, additional adults = 0.7, children less than 14 years = 0.5.
[2/] Based on a 1993 PPP rate of US$1 = 0.16 lei, inflated to May 1997 using the CPI, yielding a PPP rate of around US$1 = 0.49 and the World Bank Absolute Minimum Poverty Line of $1 per person per day and 30 days per month.
Source: Estimates based on the Moldova Household Budget Survey, 1997. February results are from the pilot of the survey, and August results are from the second round. Results for May are available as well, in Ackland (1998) in World Bank (1999).

---

[5] The empirical results in this report draw on quarterly data from the Moldovan Household Budget Survey, which had its pilot in February 1997, first round in May 1997, and second round in August 1997.

Sarkisyan minimum consumption basket, which is a generous basket reflecting Soviet-era consumption patterns, almost all Moldovans are "poor".

In order to understand the nature of poverty, and to design policy measures to address it, the overall numbers are less important than the composition of poverty according to categories of individuals and their location. As can be seen from Indicator Box 1.3, estimates of the actual number of the poor will vary from one point in time to another, depending on real factors such as economic growth and seasonality, and sampling issues. It is still useful to get a rough idea of the overall poverty indices, in order to design effective intermediation in the most appropriate way.

Employment status and poverty

In Moldova, due to the ongoing recession, employment status alone is not a significant factor in being poor, though open unemployment does increase the chances of poverty. This can be seen in Figure 1.4, (previous page) which divides the poor according to their status in the labor force. 45 percent of the poor are in the labor force (at the top of the chart)—but, of them, two out of three are employed. Therefore, being employed *per se* does not guarantee a sufficient income in Moldova to escape poverty. This is because of two factors. First, the "slackness" of the labor market in general, where only a small group of skills are in high demand and thus well-compensated. Second, the prevailing practice of many employers with inadequate resources to adjust to the recession through lowering effective pay rather than eliminating employment. Many of those who are employed work in sectors where wages have been relatively fixed over the past few years, and thus are falling sharply in real terms. Many of these employers, including some local governments, moribund industries and collective farms, also have had several months' arrears in wage payments. On the other hand, being openly unemployed can make a difference. Regression analysis of 1997 data shows that, while the labor force status of the household head does not have a significant impact on household welfare, the presence of each additional unemployed household member lowers the household's average by about 16 percent.[6]

Age and poverty

✓ **INDICATOR BOX 1.5: Children, more than the elderly, contribute to the household's poverty**

Household Composition		Measures of Poverty	
Children present	*Elderly present*	Headcount	Poverty Gap
No	No	12.6	26.9
Yes	No	29.9	33.8
No	Yes	17.0	26.3
Yes	Yes	23.7	29.6

Note: Headcounts are the weighted percentage of individuals with monthly expenditures below the relevant poverty line. The poverty gap is the percentage difference between the consumption of the poor and the poverty line. Children are 14 years and below, elderly 65 years and above.
Source: Estimates based on the Moldova Household Budget Survey, February 1997.

In Moldova, age is a significant factor in poverty, with younger people, in general, more vulnerable—particularly families with children. This is partly evident from Figure 1.4, which shows that children and the elderly together comprise 42 percent of the poor. This could be explained by the fact that they usually do not work, and thus do not contribute to earnings. But significantly, children are the single largest group among the poor, outnumbering the elderly by almost three to one.[7]

---

[6] Ackland (1998). This estimated impact of open unemployment on household welfare supports what has been found in other FSU countries.

The presence of children is thus strongly related to poverty. These results from Moldova are also supported by similar findings elsewhere in the FSU and Eastern Europe. In February 1997, 23.5 percent of all Moldovans were poor by the measures used in this study. But, as Indicator Box 1.5 shows, almost 30 percent of those in households with children, and without elderly members, were poor, and their average consumption was over one-third below the poverty line. By contrast, only 17 percent of families where the elderly were present, but not children, were poor. Of course, families that had no dependent members—either young or old— were the best off. Results from May 1997 confirm this. While about 19 percent of Moldovans were considered poor in May, individuals living in households with no children had poverty rates of 13.5 percent, while these rates increased with additional children, to 34.2 percent for individuals living in households with three or more children.

The poverty of children is explained to a great extent by the greater relative poverty of their younger parents. Children are part of relatively younger households. The workers in those households are dominated by those in their 30s, who entered the workforce at the peak of the economic transformation in Moldova and the accompanying structural recession. These younger members of the workforce have also been those that have been the most handicapped by the mismatch of their training and skills with the rapid evolution of the economy into one

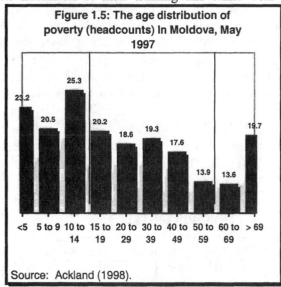

Figure 1.5: The age distribution of poverty (headcounts) in Moldova, May 1997

Source: Ackland (1998).

dominated by the market and an industrial structure jeopardized by vastly different relative prices. This is borne out by the data, as shown in Figure 1.5—of working age individuals (ages between the vertical lines in the figure), the highest incidence of poverty is among those in the 15-39 age group. More directly, as shown in Indicator Box 1.6, the poverty rates for individuals are highest where the heads of households are in the 30 to 39 age range, especially where the head is male. Yet, individuals living in households with heads aged below 30 years have a lower incidence of poverty compared to other groups. In May, the poverty rate for this group was 13.9 percent. This is encouraging, and may demonstrate that people who entered the workforce in the post-independence years have been more able to adapt their skills to the needs of the workforce.

The data also shows that households containing elderly persons do not have a higher risk of poverty—the older generation is not the most vulnerable group in Moldova—especially those in the 60-69 age group. In May 1997, the poverty rate for persons living in households with no elderly persons or only one elderly person was close to the average poverty rate of about 19 percent, while the poverty rate was 14.4 percent for those living with two or more elderly persons. Overall, the elderly, who were 17 percent of the population, were just 10.5 percent of

---

[7] The results for the age distribution of poverty have to be qualified by the fact that the calculations assume that there are no "economies of scale" in household consumption—that is, the per capita consumption of larger households with additional children does not go down with size. With larger economies of scale, the number of children who are poor may be less.

the poor.[8] These findings are also consistent with those in Russia, Ukraine and Armenia, where it was also found that the presence of elderly persons in the household does not significantly increase the risk of poverty.

This runs counter to popular opinion, which sees the elderly as among the most vulnerable in Moldova. This is partly due to the legacy of older people being among the non-workers in the population. One possibility is that senior or more well-established families might have preferential access to more or better land and housing. Perhaps as importantly, many of the elderly were able to accumulate other physical assets during their working life in Soviet times, from which they are able to get a stream of income either in cash, or more usually in kind.

Some sections of the elderly are, indeed, very poor. Those living alone, or depending exclusively on their pensions for support, may be extremely vulnerable. Those who are no longer capable of physically cultivating their land (including urban gardens) often lease their land to others, in exchange for what is sometimes a very meager portion of the harvest. Moreover, extensive intra-familial and intra-social sharing and coping arrangements also help in keeping the elderly out of poverty. As can be seen in Figure 1.5, the data for May 1997 shows the incidence of poverty rising sharply for those aged 70 and above—almost entirely due to an increase in the poverty rate for women. Data from August 1997 suggests that this increase in vulnerability for the elderly may not be as sharp.[9]

Overall, poverty in Moldova tends to decline with age, with an increase in vulnerability at more advanced ages. This result is confirmed

✓ **INDICATOR BOX 1.6: Poverty is highest in families where the household head is in his or her 30s, or a female in her 60s**

Age range	Male (% poor)	Female (% poor)
<30 years	14.8	15.1
30-39	22.8	16.9
40-49	19.2	13.4
50-59	18.1	18.5
60-69	14.4	23.8
>=70	15.4	31.4
Total	18.9	19.3

Note: Data for May 1997. Magnitudes for August 1997 vary, but the trends for age-groups 30-69 are similar. However, there is no sharp increase in poverty for households headed by females over 70, and much lower poverty for households headed by women below 30.
Source: Ackland (1997).

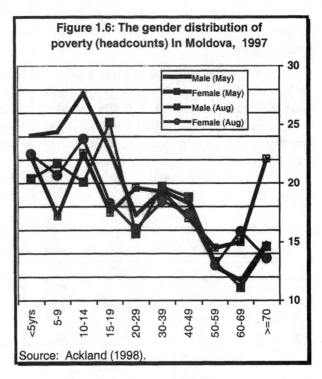

Figure 1.6: The gender distribution of poverty (headcounts) In Moldova, 1997

Male (May)
Female (May)
Male (Aug)
Female (Aug)

Source: Ackland (1998).

---

[8] This finding is consistent with results from other former socialist and communist countries (including Russia, Ukraine, Armenia, Kyrgyzstan, Azerbaijan, Estonia and countries in Eastern Europe).

[9] The poverty headcounts for May 1997 were 13.6 for ages 60-69, and 19.7 for 70 and above. The corresponding results for August were 13.6 and 13.9 respectively.

by regression analysis, which shows that the age of the household head is positively correlated with household welfare.[10] It is also evident from Figure 1.5, and the greater detail in Figure 1.6 and Indicator Box 1.5. Individuals living in households with heads aged 30-39 years had a poverty rate of 22.8 percent. For households headed by males over the age of 40, the individual poverty rate then declines slowly with the head's age. However, for individuals living in households headed by females over the age of 40, the poverty rate begins to increase with the head's age. The finding that individuals living in households with young heads have a lower incidence of poverty suggests that young people may be more adept at adjusting to changing labor market conditions.

Gender and poverty

Generally, women have a lower incidence of poverty than men, but the pattern reverses among the elderly. As Figure 1.6 shows, women and men of working age have generally similar rates of poverty, which apparently illustrates the relatively equal earning opportunities in Moldova. There is much higher variance, however, at both ends of the age scale. Clearly, both sets of observations (in May and in August) show the increased vulnerability of women compared to men as they get older. There does not seem to be a definite pattern from the data as to the relative poverty of girls compared to boys. However, it should be emphasized that the apparent lack of a gender dimension to poverty in Moldova (and in other countries) may in part be due to methodology, since the household survey does not provide information on the distribution of consumption within a household. The accompanying assumption—that all household members receive an equal share—is contradicted by anthropological studies for Moldova that show that women tend to give themselves the lowest priority when dividing up food for meals.[11]

The gender of the household head does, however, affect the poverty of individuals in the households. Consumption regressions with the 1997 data show that households with female heads have an estimated per capita consumption that is 9.8 percent lower than those in comparable households headed by males. This result, however, is driven mostly by the large increases in poverty in households headed by women in their sixties. In May 1997, such households had a poverty headcount of 23.8 percent, compared with 19 percent for the economy as a whole, and just 14.4 percent for households headed by men in the same age group.

✓ **INDICATOR BOX 1.7: Poverty is highest and most severe in rural areas in Moldova**

	May 1997			Aug. 1997		
	P0	P1	P2	P0	P1	P2
Chisinau	6.9	1.5	0.6	6.7	1.8	0.7
Other cities	16.8	4.5	1.7	17.2	4.7	1.9
Rural areas	23.3	8.2	4.2	21.1	6.9	3.4
Overall	19.0	6.2	3.1	17.9	5.6	2.7

Note: P0, the headcount index is defined as the percentage of people who are poor. P1, the poverty gap index measures the average difference of per capita consumption from the poverty line. P2, the severity of poverty, gives greater weight to those with per capita consumption further from the poverty line.
Source: Ackland (1997).

---

[10] Braithwaite (1997) and Ackland (1998).

WHERE ARE THE POOR?

GEOGRAPHICAL AND SECTORAL DISTRIBUTION

The rural-urban divide

The relative number of poor people is much greater in rural Moldova compared to urban areas, and is markedly low in Chisinau compared to the rest of the country. Overall, the incidence of poverty in Moldova (calculated over individuals) was 17.9 percent in August 1997. However, the rural poverty rate was 21.1 percent, compared with only 6.7 percent in Chisinau and 17.2 percent in other cities (the corresponding numbers for May are similar, and both are shown in Indicator Box 1.7).

Moreover, poverty in rural areas was particularly deep and severe as compared to urban centers, and especially when compared to Chisinau. The depth of poverty is measured by the "poverty gap"—the average difference between the consumption of the poor and the poverty line consumption, as seen in Indicator Box 1.7. This was also significantly greater in rural areas. On average, the consumption of a rural poor person was one-and-a-half times distant from the poverty line than that of her counterpart in urban centers other than Chisinau, and almost four times than that of a poor person in Chisinau. Similar results were found for the severity of poverty (which puts greater weight on relatively poorer people). Poverty was much less severe in Chisinau. That is, even the poorer people in Chisinau were clustered much closer to the poverty line than were poor people in rural areas.

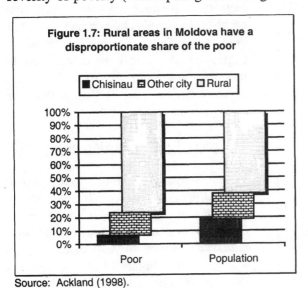

Figure 1.7: Rural areas in Moldova have a disproportionate share of the poor

Source: Ackland (1998).

A different way to look at the same issue is to look at the distribution of poverty. This also varies markedly by type of location, as can be seen in Figure 1.7. While 18.7 percent of the population live in Chisinau, only 6.8 percent of the poor in Moldova live there. By contrast, 62.0 percent of individuals live in rural areas, yet rural poverty accounts for 76.1 percent of all poor.

The fact that rural poverty is higher than poverty in Chisinau is consistent with findings from other countries. In most other FSU countries, the rural poverty rate is indeed higher than that for the major city. This is because economic activity is generally

VOICES: A collective farm worker (1)

"A family does not starve if at least one member works in the collective farm."

—de Soto and Dudwick (1997)

---

[11] See, for instance, de Soto and Dudwick (1997).

---

concentrated in the major city, and therefore employment and earnings opportunities are greater than in rural areas. Moreover, in the case of Moldova, Chisinau has been the sole engine of growth (in 1997, Chisinau grew by around 10 percent, fueled by a construction boom, while Moldova overall had just a 1.3 percent growth).

The finding that rural poverty rates are higher than those for 'other' urban areas (i.e. urban areas which are not the capital or major city) runs contrary to findings in other FSU countries, and may be partly explained by the access of urban Moldovans to the rural food surplus. In the FSU, rural residents may find themselves better off than those living in other urban areas due to their ability to consume food that is home produced (i.e., grown in a garden plot or produced on a farm).[12] The converse finding in Moldova may be due to a combination of two reasons. One may be purely statistical, as the Moldova household survey relies on self-reported valuations for home consumption, which may have led to an under-valuation of home consumption.[13] A second reason, however, may be the fairly widespread ownership of dacha plots in the countryside by urban Moldovans, the frequent travel to the countryside by urban dwellers (especially in summer) and the continuing close ties with family in rural areas.[14] Ownership of household plots, as a source of food for self-consumption, has also been increasing over time, from 8.3 percent of all agricultural land in 1990 to 13.1 percent in 1997.[15] As a result, there is no marked relative disadvantage in terms of consumption to living in urban areas.

One difference with the past, however, is the ability of poor families to smooth their consumption over the seasons. In pre-independence years, families enjoyed not only fresh fruits and vegetables, but canned and preserved their own produce or that which they purchased cheaply in summer and fall. Poor households can no longer afford sugar, can lids, or in some cases, even the fuel for preserving the food. They can preserve with salt rather than with sugar, and in far smaller quantities than before.

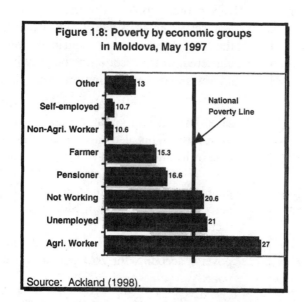

Figure 1.8: Poverty by economic groups in Moldova, May 1997

Other 13
Self-employed 10.7
Non-Agri. Worker 10.6
Farmer 15.3
Pensioner 16.6
Not Working 20.6
Unemployed 21
Agri. Worker 27

National Poverty Line

Source: Ackland (1998).

The sectoral distribution of poverty

Mirroring the geographical distribution described above, agricultural workers (as opposed to farmers) are occupationally the most vulnerable group in Moldova. This is illustrated in Figure 1.8. Moreover, individuals in households where the heads were extremely poor had poverty rates of 27.2 and 24.6 in May and August 1997, respectively. The slow progress in structural transformation in Moldovan agriculture is an explanation.

---

[12] See, for example, Braithwaite, 1997a.

[13] This has been found in other countries such as Russia.

[14] Some urban dwellers received land plots allocated for housing, in lieu of apartments, and some of those who didn't build on them now grow vegetables there. Others cultivate unclaimed patches of urban land, which they fence when disputes arise. On the outskirts of Chisinau, people have larger lots which they use for farming (de Soto and Dudwick 1997).

[15] See Figure 2.4 in the next chapter.

Moldova, unlike the countries in the Caucasus, did not undergo land reform in the early years since independence. In 1997, most farms were still unreformed kolkhozi (collective farms) or sovkhozi (State farms). With Soviet input and output channels in disarray, and existing sales mostly in barter, the farms are chronically unable to pay wages to workers, especially in cash.[16],[17] The findings, described earlier in this chapter, about the emergence of a large class of "working poor", are also generated by these workers. The few private farmers (landowners) who had emerged by 1997 were able to respond relatively well to the structural changes in the economy, and were thus better off than their landless compatriots.

Non-agricultural workers and the self-employed have the lowest chance of being poor. The finding that self-employed are doing relatively well supports evidence from other FSU countries, although the low poverty rates among non-agricultural workers is an encouraging sign of the relatively more rapid adjustment in the industrial and service sectors in Moldova. This also correlates with the geographical finding that poverty rates are lower in Chisinau and other urban centers, where non-agricultural employment dominates.

VOICES: A collective farm worker (2)

"Only God knows how we shall survive over winter. My family only has milk if the collective farms pay us in milk instead of cash, or if someone from the village gives milk to my son for a share of his salary as a shepherd. But this is rare. We can't afford to spend our monthly salary only on milk. And if we agreed with the collective farm managers to get milk, we would only receive milk and no salary."

–de Soto and Dudwick (1997)

Of those outside the workforce, unemployment has a clear correlation with poverty, but pensioners are not especially vulnerable. Persons who are unemployed had a relatively high poverty incidence—and regression analysis for the May data found a significant link between the number of unemployed household members and household welfare.[18] As in other FSU countries, pensioners in Moldova do not have a higher than average incidence of poverty, a result that is confirmed for individuals in households headed by a pensioner.

WHAT DO THE POOR OWN?

HUMAN CAPITAL, ASSET OWNERSHIP AND POVERTY

The role of educational endowments

The ownership of assets—either human capital in the form of education, or tangible, physical assets such as land—has a major bearing on poverty status in Moldova. Ownership of both types of assets help to provide their owners with a stream of income—and thus one would expect that those who were either highly educated, or owned sufficient amounts of land,

---

[16] Moldovan farms are being aggressively reformed since 1997, with almost 150 ex-collective farms now broken down and individual titles given to farmers. As will be discussed later, the emergence of a new class of private farmers from the former wage-workers is gradually improving earnings ability in the rural sector. Current plans are to complete the restructuring of most of Moldova's almost 900 large farms by the end of 2000.

[17] de Soto and Dudwick (1997) describe a farm near Balti that worked out a trade agreement with farms in Belarus, where they traded apples for spare parts and fertilizers.

[18] See Ackland (1998).

would be more likely to be able to escape poverty.

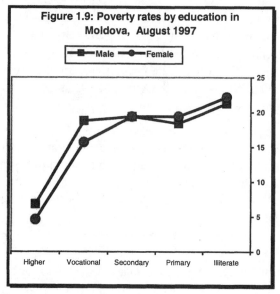

Source: Ackland (1998).

Results from the Moldovan data do confirm this hypothesis.

The return to education—both of the individual and of the household head—is remarkably high in Moldova. Figure 1.9 shows the numbers for August 1997—a monotonically increasing relationship between incidence of poverty and lower educational attainment of individuals aged 14 years and over. In May, the profile was similar—the poverty rate for a person with higher education was 7.3 percent compared with 25.8 percent for an illiterate person. This phenomenon is also evident in the relationship between poverty status and education of household heads. In May, individuals living in households headed by a person with higher education had a poverty rate of 6.3 percent, compared with 26.8 percent for individuals living in households headed by persons who are illiterate.

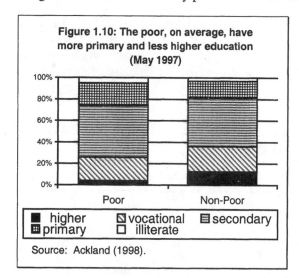

Source: Ackland (1998).

The data show relatively low returns to education between primary and secondary/vocational education, but a large difference between those who are illiterate versus those with some formal schooling. Persons with vocational/technical or general secondary/incomplete secondary education have poverty rates generally around the average—showing that this does not accord them either a particular advantage or disadvantage in Moldova's labor market. In particular, much of vocational education has low payoffs, as the decline in traditional industries in Moldova has resulted in a fall in demand for workers with pre-transition technical qualifications. The higher poverty of the illiterate, while expected, is interesting given that Moldova, as a former Soviet economy, had almost universal primary education. Most of the relatively less literate, therefore, either live in deeply rural areas, or are older, with their educational history a relic of the earlier part of the century.

The return to higher education is very high in Moldova. The very small poverty rates for those with higher education is consistent with the fact that people with higher education in Moldova also have lower unemployment rates.[19] This is borne out by regression results on consumption, which show that household heads having a higher education degree are associated

---

[19] Lindauer, 1998.

with per capita household consumption being 36.3 percent higher than in a household where the head has primary/incomplete primary education.[20] As is shown by Figure 1.10, the converse is true as well—people from poor households are less likely to have higher education (only 4.7 percent of poor individuals have a higher degree, compared with 13.4 percent of the non-poor).

Inter-generationally, the children of today's poor have a chance of remaining poor in adulthood, since poverty has a clear effect of lowering their ability to educate themselves. A study of education in Moldova using the pilot data from February for the Household Survey found marked differences in enrolment rates between poor and non-poor children.[21] Perhaps surprisingly, the difference was higher in Chisinau and other urban areas—in Chisinau, the enrolment rate of poor children was over 20 percentage points lower than that of non-poor children. This suggests that unless policies are designed to allow poor children to accumulate human capital, the gap in earning power between the poor and non-poor is likely to increase in Moldova's future, thus making it even more difficult for the poor to improve their standard of living.

Ownership of garden plots

✓ **INDICATOR BOX 1.8: Garden plots enable their owners to escape poverty**

% poor	Urban	Rural	All
No plot	11.7	24.4	19.9
Owns plot	13.0	14.7	13.8
Total	12.0	23.3	19.0

Source: Ackland (1998).
Note: Data for May 1997.

PERSPECTIVES: Garden plots
Although many subsistence farmers ostensibly are members of a restructured collective farm, it is their .30 hectare land plots that provide their basic subsistence. For some who contemplate farming as a way of life, this experience has provided a transition to independent farming; for others it is a stopgap which only supplements their income. For still others, it has suggested a way to not only provide basic subsistence, but even earn a predictable income, through the establishment of greenhouses, for example.
--de Soto and Dudwick (1997)

Access to a garden plot makes a clear difference in the ability of Moldovans to improve their standard of living, but the impact is much greater in rural areas. In May 1997, 17.4 percent of urban households and 11.6 percent of rural households owned garden plots, using them to grow produce mainly for self-consumption. The data for May shows that individuals living in households with access to a garden plot had an incidence of poverty of 13.8 percent, compared to the average poverty rate of 19.0 percent. But the ownership of plots made a significant difference in poverty rates only in rural households, who were able to use home plots to mitigate poverty. As can be seen in Indicator Box 1.8, the poverty rate for individuals in rural areas with access to a garden plot was nearly half that found for persons with no access to a plot. There is not much difference in urban poverty rates between those who had access to a food plot and those who did not. This may be

---

[20] Ackland (1998).

[21] Ackland (1997).

because income from sources other than self-consumption (mostly labor income) played a much larger role in urban households than in rural ones.[22]

VOICES: A pensioner

"The mayor promised in the last elections that he was going to give us gas and hot water, but since the whole town has been privatized, we don't have anything. I cook on a single electric plate."
--de Soto and Dudwick (1997)

Utilities, durable goods and poverty

Living conditions were also much worse for the poor as compared to non-poor households. As can be seen in Indicator Box 1.9, there are clear differences in the presence of utilities and ownership of durable goods between poor and non-poor households. In May, non-poor households were about twice as likely as poor households to have most utilities (except that the non-poor were two-and-a-half times as likely to have hot water). This may be a manifestation of the fact that most of Moldova's poor (as seen in Figure 1.7 earlier) live in rural areas, where utility connections are not as universal as in urban areas. A partial confirmation of this also comes from the fact that the non-poor are more than two-and-a-half times as likely to live in an apartment (more prevalent in urban areas) than in a separate house (the usual form of accommodation in Moldova's rural areas).

✓ **INDICATOR BOX 1.9: The poor have much less access to either utilities or durables**

% Households with:	Poor	Non-poor	% Households with:	Poor	Non-poor
Sewerage	17.0	35.1	Color TV	20.6	40.1
Hot water	9.3	25.2	VCR	1.6	5.4
Central gas	13.6	30.9	Refrigerator	64.8	73.6
Central heating	18.3	36.3	Washing machine	43.5	55.2
Bath or shower	14.9	33.1	Car	6.3	11.8
Phone	18.4	34.9			

% Households with:	Poor	Non-poor
Separate apartment	12.4	29.2
Separate house	79.2	62.3

Source: Household Budget Survey data, May 1997, calculated by Ackland (1998).

The poor in Moldova also possess fewer durables, especially those that have become more common over the last decade (Indicator Box 1.9). Since the household survey did not discriminate across the age or quality of durable goods, it is difficult to compare them across poor and non-poor sections of the population. The non-poor are clearly more likely to own a VCR, a color television and a car. The latter is of importance in coping strategies, since car ownership may help in providing an income stream, especially in urban areas.

---

[22] These results are supported by anthropological evidence and regression analysis (de Soto and Dudwick 1997 and Ackland 1998) respectively. Ackland shows that ownership of land is a key determinant of cash income and consumption of food, especially in rural areas. The presence of a food plot is associated with a 10.6 percent increase in per capita consumption.

TOOL BOX 1.10: Choosing a poverty line for Moldova

Conceptually, poverty is the inability to sustain some minimal level of existence. Yet defining that "minimal" level, especially when money income may not give a good measure of real consumption opportunities, is problematic. A standard approach to defining an absolute level of poverty is to price a basket of essential goods and compare income to the cost of these necessities. But both in the definition of nutritional needs and the calculation of corresponding cost, value judgments occur on the part of experts or the politicians deciding on a certain method, and the reliability of conclusions formed on this basis depend critically on the reliability of the income information to which it is compared.

In the Soviet period, even data for providing the food component of an absolute poverty line were scarce, and Moldova and other FSU countries inherited a concept of a "minimal consumer basket" that was not minimalist in any sense. The actual basket contained over 250 norms for the consumption of food and non-food goods, including alcohol and tobacco, and a "normed rate" of savings. This basket is inappropriate for truly determining vulnerability in Moldova or indeed, in any other FSU country today. This report does use an absolute poverty line, but one that is based on a consumer basket of 2100 calories a day, with added non-food consumption that is typical for families at that level of food consumption.

Moreover, in Moldova, as in almost all other countries, households do not fully disclose their income to survey interviewers or the tax authorities. Indeed, in every World Bank assessment of poverty in a FSU country to date, this under-reporting has resulted in reported expenditures considerably exceeding reported income. Since the goal of poverty analysis is to assess the real welfare of households and the people who comprise them, expenditure can be a better measure of household consumption than income. Such expenditure aggregates can be constructed to include the self-reported value of food produced on a household's private plot of land, and also the consumption of food or other goods received in kind by the household.

As a result, a relative poverty line was chosen for this first attempt at examining who is poor in Moldova. The relative poverty line adopted was 40 percent of the unweighted mean per capita consumption. This particular line was used for one very practical reason--it was available immediately while the versions of population weights were being finalized. Using the population-weighted mean per capita consumption would lead to a slightly lower poverty line and therefore a lower headcount. Neither line is "right" or "wrong"--they are merely different.

2. POVERTY, PRICES AND INCOMES

The poverty of individuals and households in Moldova have mirrored the causes of the overall slowdown in the economy. Many enterprises found that the post-Soviet economic structure resulted in a vast increase in the ratio of their input prices to the market price of their output. Similarly, consumers found that the market prices of necessities—food and especially energy—were relatively (and in a few cases, absolutely) greater than the price their labor could fetch in the new recessionary labor market. Unemployment and underemployment have been climbing, but a closer examination of the composition of the unemployed shows that the majority of them are in rural areas, in the 25 to 50 age group, and with just secondary education—and the incidence of poverty is relatively high among the unemployed. These are precisely the groups that are also the most vulnerable to poverty. To eradicate poverty over the medium term, therefore, there is a need for employment-generating growth, which has to primarily come from the effects of the large-scale restructuring now going on in Moldova's agricultural sector. Over the medium term, this will also come from a change in the composition and growth pattern of the service sector in Moldova.

The process of transition created a macro environment that is not necessarily supportive to employment generation and growth unless accompanied by fundamental structural adjustment. As shown in Figure 2.1, hyperinflation, and a period of sharp adjustment from the hyperinflation, marked the initial phase of transition. Moldova was one of the stars among FSU countries in having an early, and drastic, adjustment, reducing its annual inflation rate from 1,276 percent in 1992 to just 30 percent by 1995, the lowest among the CIS countries. The adjustment assured a renewed faith in the domestic currency, and a slowdown in the erosion of the assets of the poor and those who lived on fixed incomes. However, the drastic monetary and credit contraction that

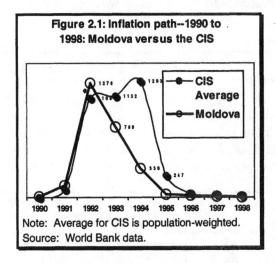

Figure 2.1: Inflation path--1990 to 1998: Moldova versus the CIS

Note: Average for CIS is population-weighted.
Source: World Bank data.

fueled the adjustment was not accompanied by fundamental fiscal and structural reforms—there was initially no fundamental restructuring of public expenditures, not much progress in land reform, and little restructuring of enterprises. Therefore, the initial set of reforms, though necessary at the time, were far from sufficient in providing the conditions for growth in employment and incomes.

Nominal incomes were greatly eroded by the hyperinflation in 1992 and thereafter. With the slowdown in growth, they have remained at very low real levels since—with many public

---

VOICES: An elderly pensioner
"[Before independence] I had two thousand rubles saved in the bank for a rainy day, for my funeral. It was quite enough during those times. Now I have two lei. What can I buy with them?"
– de Soto and Dudwick (1997)

---

employees (such as teachers) receiving under US$20 a month for their services. For many families, the drastic erosion of pre-independence savings has also caused increased insecurities about the future, and reduced their ability to manage variations in their income streams.

Enterprises, as employers, have also been affected by changing relative prices of inputs and market conditions. Both agricultural (*kolkhozi* and *sovkhozi*) and industrial enterprises have found themselves less able to produce (due to the high cost of imported raw material, including energy). Even if they do produce, they are less able to sell their goods in a trading system that is no longer as predictable as in Soviet times. As a result, most enterprises no longer have the surpluses to pay their workers' wages or to subsidize their needs. Some have resorted to layoffs. Many (especially those still owned by the State) have kept their workers officially on the rolls, but have either put them on unpaid leave or have accumulated wage arrears, sometimes for months on end. Again, some have stopped providing social services to their employees by divesting themselves of social assets—but most have retained the institutions that provide service to their workers, but lack of funds have made these services either low quality or effectively unavailable. The Government itself, still a significant employer in Moldova (especially in the health and education sectors), has faced the same problem. For the public sector, this has manifested itself in the low wages for public employees described above.

The challenge in terms of lowering poverty is to put into place sufficient processes that would create economic growth that generates employment and raises wages. This chapter will examine the role of relative prices, and then the operation of the labor market in greater detail, as a precursor to understanding what the Government's policy options are.

RELATIVE PRICE SHOCKS AND THE POOR

The poor in Moldova have faced two different shocks—the first an "income shock" as their earning ability declined in the new economy, and the second a "price shock" as the relative price of consumables rose sharply compared to the price of their output. In today's Moldova, the most important items in the consumption basket are food and energy costs. While food prices have increased greatly since pre-independence days, Moldovans have been able to hedge against these increases by switching their consumption to cheaper products or those that they can produce themselves. It has been difficult, however, to adjust to the shock of extremely large rises in energy prices, especially the cost of district heating for urban Moldovans.

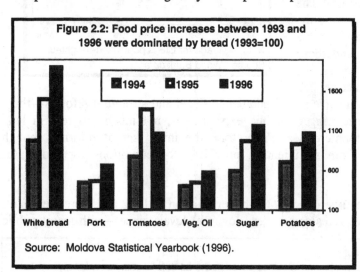

Figure 2.2: Food price increases between 1993 and 1996 were dominated by bread (1993=100)

Source: Moldova Statistical Yearbook (1996).

Moldova, as an agricultural producer, has been able to protect its consumers reasonably well against increases in food prices—and thus food-related poverty is still relatively low. Food is by far the largest item of consumption for the poor. In May 1997, food and beverages were 82.5 percent of the consumption of the poor (as opposed to 67.9 percent of consumption for all Moldovans). The moderation in food prices has been especially true due to the economy-wide price stabilization since 1995, but has also been because of the large amount of self-production of food. Due to this, before independence, the majority of people were able to feed their families adequately, if not sumptuously. Moreover, they had enough from incomes, pensions, and allowances to purchase what they did not grow.

Other agricultural prices, though not necessarily subsidized, were affordable, since most consumers in this heavily agricultural country were also part of the production chain (either directly or indirectly). In more recent years, and particularly in the latter half of 1998, food prices have also been driven down greatly by the loss of traditional export markets, especially Russia. As a result, there has been an excess supply of food to the domestic market (especially Chisinau), driving prices down greatly. Given the relative abundance of agricultural commodities, consumers were also able to switch fairly easily between products within food groups as the within-group relative prices changed—the switch by the poor away from bread (mentioned below) being a good example.

Most food production was indirectly subsidized through cheap inputs including energy and transportation. The major directly subsidized food product was bread. As can be seen in Figure 2.2, the removal of the bread subsidy had the largest single effect on people's food baskets, which are dominated (Figure 2.3) by grain products. The price of bread rose from 0.09 lei in 1993 to 1.72 lei in 1996. The poor in Moldova today subsist much more heavily on *mamaliga* (corn meal) and potatoes for their staple starch. These products are also subject to the vagaries of the agricultural cycle. For example, the potato harvest was poor in 1996, and retail prices rose to about 1.50 lei per kg. Large families, which consume 400-500 kg of potatoes a year, would have required 600-700 lei, then an impossible sum for cash-poor families.

The market has not yet fully captured the full price adjustment for food products, and therefore further price changes may be in the offing. In 1996, for example, potatoes were not exported, and the production costs for potatoes were even higher than the domestic retail price— about 2.45 lei per kg versus 0.93 lei to the producer and 1.50 lei at the market.[1] Domestic producer prices for vegetables in 1996 were 71 percent of production costs, though exported vegetables fetched a 25 percent premium. As export markets recover, therefore, consumers in Moldova may have to face world prices, which would often be higher than the prices they pay in a more segmented market.

The largest change in relative prices faced by Moldova, and more recently by Moldovans, has been in energy costs. Moldova, which imports almost all of its energy in the form of gas and electricity from Russia and Ukraine respectively, had long enjoyed subsidized prices for the energy. It paid

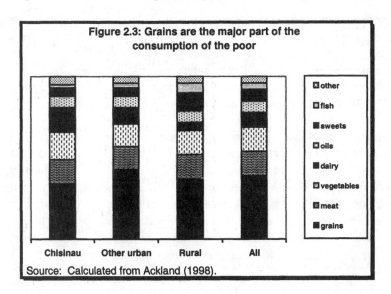

Figure 2.3: Grains are the major part of the consumption of the poor

other
fish
sweets
oils
dairy
vegetables
meat
grains

Chisinau   Other urban   Rural   All

Source: Calculated from Ackland (1998).

---

[1] Moldova Statistical Yearbook (1996).

for energy imports with exports of agricultural and other goods. With the breakdown of Soviet trading practices, the price of energy has risen significantly. Between 1995 and 1997, the price of electricity to consumers rose by around 15 percent. Then, faced by a ruinous external debt due to energy non-payments and underpayments, the Government was forced, in June 1997, to initiate a series of major price increases. For electricity, household tariffs rose again by more than 20 percent. At the same time, household tariffs for gas rose by 40 percent. Most drastic was the increase in district heating tariffs, by about 90 percent over previous levels. In late 1998, the tariff for heating increased again, by a further 60 percent.

The price and availability of fuel for heating is a serious problem for Moldovans. Most dwellings in Chisinau and other major towns are heated from the central system. Consumers complain, though, that the heat provided is often inadequate, and the temperature is unregulated.[2] For the producers, on the other hand, non-payment is a serious problem. For one, with the recent increase in heating prices, the cost of heating a two-bedroom apartment is equivalent to the salary of an average wage-earner—so the ability to pay for heat is usually absent. The willingness to pay for heat is also an issue, given the poor quality of the service, and the fact that non-payers cannot be easily cut off from the system. For the consumers who do pay, the lack of technological options to opt out of the system presents the problem that they are less able to make the investment in alternative sources of heating in winter. Usually, therefore, if district heating is not adequate, consumers rely on portable heaters, or, if that is unaffordable, on keeping the stove on. The Government has attempted to compensate households for the increase in the price for district heating by instituting a somewhat targeted, though still generous, "lifeline" tariff system, and is now undertaking major changes in the system of compensating the poor for energy price increases. This system will be discussed in more detail in Chapter 3, but would need an improvement in targeting over the short run, and the creation of incentives to move away from unaffordable centralized heating over the medium term.

In rural areas, coal used to be a common form of fuel, and is still supplied at a discount to pensioners. Yet, many families cannot spend the US$200-250 for two tons of (often poor quality) coal required to heat a home for the winter. Even pensioners, entitled to free or discounted coal, have not always received their allocation in time—and, when they have, often lack the 30-40 lei needed to have their 500-kg entitlement transported to their apartment.

Most families try to pay their electricity bills, since those unable to do so often have their service cut. Yet, despite the price of electricity, many families still resort to electric heaters and hot plates for cooking because they no longer receive natural gas. But power brownouts are common, and have been increasingly so over the past year when external payment problems reduced the supply of energy to Moldova. Although brownouts are rarer in Chisinau, some rural communities receive power for only two hours in the morning and two hours in the evening.

The Government has responded to the inability of consumers to meet high energy prices by attempting to compensate them for the price increase. As will be discussed in the next chapter, these attempts, while well meaning, are unsustainable. For one, they are fiscally unaffordable for a Government every bit as cash-poor as some of its citizens. Second, they need to be better targeted towards the poor, so as not to direct scarce resources to the less deserving in the population. Most important, the rise in energy prices, although significant in absolute terms, does not place a major effective burden on the poor. Most poor, pressed to meet their food needs, either avoid paying for energy or, in rarer cases, go without to the extent that they can.

---

[2] The usual temperature regulating method in most apartments is the degree to which windows are kept open in winter.

THE LABOR MARKET AS A SOURCE OF INCOME

Changes in the labor market and the economic environment have driven the radical changes in the composition of the poor in Moldova since Soviet days. In Soviet times, the poor were usually just the disabled, the criminal or the pensioners—that is, those (at least in theory) who were unable or unwilling to work. Employment at a minimum of a living wage was assured for all people of working age, regardless of their absolute productivity or ability. The employer and the State, in addition, provided the Soviet worker and his or her family with subsidized or free housing, energy, education, child care, health care and even, in some cases, with food and other consumables. Therefore, although some were always relatively worse off than others, absolute deprivation was rare among working families. In its turn, the State provided assistance for those who were unable to work, through old age pensions and disability payments. As will be pointed out later, in Chapter 3, the legacy of this system of social protection still continues in today's Moldova, but is unable to protect the real poor.

Therefore, the new labor market in Moldova has confronted individuals with paradoxes. On the one hand, people are accustomed to and feel better with permanent, full time jobs and salaries. On the other hand, salaries from regular employment are often received with great delay, while short-term, intermittent work generally produces an immediate return.

Overall labor dynamics

The lack of employment generation opportunities in Moldova is a facet of transition, in that job losses have outpaced the rate of job creation in the new economy. Economic transition requires job destruction in the state sector, where bloated and unproductive enterprises must be closed or, at least, dismiss redundant workers. In the case of Moldova, although many enterprises are no longer fully-owned by the State, there has not been a process of corporate ownership that would force the unpalatable layoff process. As a result, there has been rising unemployment and falling participation rates among older workers. Figure 2.4 shows an example from the Czech Republic, where, between 1991 and 1995 (the time of its transition) employment flowed from traditional sectors such as industry, agriculture, transport and health and education—mostly to commerce, construction, public administration and services. The engine of service sector growth, therefore, drove the transition. In Moldova's case, there has been no such engine of employment growth.

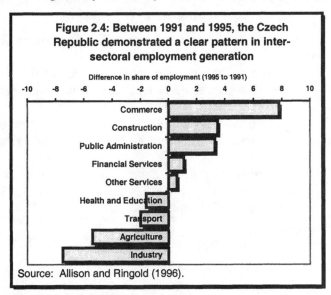

Figure 2.4: Between 1991 and 1995, the Czech Republic demonstrated a clear pattern in inter-sectoral employment generation

Difference in share of employment (1995 to 1991)

Source: Allison and Ringold (1996).

Creation of productive employment opportunities is crucial to poverty alleviation and renewed economic growth in Moldova. This does not, of course, imply that governments should go back to creating employment or sustaining jobs in state enterprises that are not commercially viable. An artificially low unemployment rate is clearly not evidence of superior economic performance. When low unemployment is the result of maintaining large numbers of workers in unproductive jobs, social welfare is compromised. In the short run, transfers from abroad or domestic inflationary financing can keep unemployment rates low, but this is a poor long run strategy for raising standards of living. What is required instead is to create conditions for the expansion of employment opportunities where there is sufficient demand for labor to raise wages of Moldova's workers from the very low levels to which they have fallen (Comparator Box 2.1).

Overall, the process of transition in Moldova's labor market has implied a reduction in both wages and employment in the public and quasi-public sectors, while there has been only a slow increase in private sector employment. Although many Moldovans are employed, they may not make enough at their official job to make ends meet. This is especially because, in many enterprises, wages are not paid regularly, but only in times when there are enough resources.

The collapse of public sector employment and the emergence of new labor niches have affected men and women differently. In public sector work, both men and women have lost jobs in production, while lower paying jobs in the social sector, such as teaching and medicine, have become almost completely dominated by women. In the private sector, as public and corporate provision of child care has declined, pregnant women and mothers have found themselves more vulnerable than men. Economic necessity has also pushed women into enterprises, some involving travel, that have simultaneously given them an independent income and therefore more autonomy.

> ★ **COMPARATOR BOX 2.1: Moldova's average wage (in US$) was one of the lowest in Europe and Central Asia in 1996**
>
> | Country | Avg. wage | Country | Avg. wage |
> |---|---|---|---|
> | Azerbaijan | 21 | Kazakhstan | 102 |
> | Armenia | 23 | Russia | 154 |
> | Kyrgyzstan | 38 | Lithuania | 156 |
> | **Moldova** | **40** | Estonia | 192 |
> | Uzbekistan | 54 | Macedonia | 181 |
> | Ukraine | 84 | Hungary | 213 |
> | Bulgaria | 72 | Czech Rep. | 341 |
> | Romania | 88 | Croatia | 363 |
> | Belarus | 89 | Poland | 372 |
>
> Source: Kuddo (1998) for CIS (*in italics*), and IMF for non-CIS countries.

Most workers who are able to earn a sufficient income in modern Moldova are in the private sector, and fall into three categories:

➤ those of the workers who are fortunate enough to be employed in one of the few existing enterprises (public or private) that were able to adapt successfully to the new market economy;

➤ the few of the younger workers who had or developed the skills (in foreign languages, computers, finance or construction) that were in greatest demand in the Moldovan economy in transition; and

➤ those, young and old, with the entrepreneurial skills to develop new businesses and activities to take advantage of the increasing opportunities for private activity in Moldova—in agriculture, in manufacturing and in trade.

VOICES: Worker at Bucuria candy factory
"When we receive more orders, I make 300-400 lei a month; sometimes I get nothing at all for several months in a row."
– de Soto and Dudwick (1997)

Wages in Moldova have not recovered from the drastic erosion caused by the hyperinflation of the early 1990s. In January 1997, the average monthly wage (reported by the State Department of Statistics' monthly survey of enterprises employing 20 or more workers) was 190 lei. Deflating by Moldova's consumer price index yields a real wage of about half of the level prevailing five years earlier, in January 1992. Most of this loss occurred in 1993. Since then, real wages have been stagnant, although there is evidence of a slight upturn in mean earnings during the latter part of 1996 and into 1997, and, from journalistic evidence, a sharp fall as inflation picked up again in the latter half of 1998 into 1999.[3,4]

Even with extremely low wages, most Moldovans prefer to be employed. For some, it is the only source of cash to supplement subsistence gardening and other items acquired through barter. Those near retirement age may also feel psychologically protected by having a job, feeling that finding other work would be unlikely. In other cases, jobs are linked to housing. Although state-funded construction has stopped, poorer people remain on job-linked waiting lists for housing still hoping to acquire an apartment in this way. Many of the poor continue to live in

---

TOOL BOX 2.2: Are labor market inflexibilities the cause of bad outcomes in Moldova?

Moldova's double-digit unemployment and large decline in real wages are serious concerns that warrant the attention of policy makers. These outcomes are problems of the labor market in the narrow sense that they are the result of interactions between labor demand and supply. But in a broader sense, there is little evidence that the operation of the labor market, per se, is to blame. The labor market in Moldova is working well within its given constraints.

Wages appear flexible as evidenced by the fall in their real value and increasing pay differentials across sectors. In January 1997, average reported monthly wages in the highest paid sector, the financial sector (704 lei), were four and a half times the level in education (155 lei), one of the lowest paid sectors. In 1992, the ratio was only 2.6:1. The minimum wage, which can limit wage flexibility and the growth of labor demand, is not a binding constraint in Moldova's labor market. When set in January of 1994, at 18 lei per month, the legal minimum appears below the market determined wage for unskilled work. Similarly, excessive payroll taxes can serve as a disincentive to employers for hiring workers. Although employment-based tax rates in Moldova are high, at present, these do not seem an important impediment to job creation. Evasion is widespread and employers find ways of designing employment contracts to avoid payments. Reform of these taxes will be warranted once the economy starts to grow but current labor taxes are not the reason for poor labor outcomes.

Other dimensions of the labor market appear to function well. Unemployment cannot be explained by a mismatch of skills and opportunities. Moldova has a well-educated and experienced labor force. Its skills are in demand abroad as evidenced by the success Moldovans have had landing legal employment contracts in, for example, Israel, and illegal guest work in Russia and neighboring countries.

The operation of the labor market does not appear as a constraint to generating jobs and rewarding workers. The constraints lie elsewhere. What is needed are institutional reforms that will make Moldova an attractive environment for private investment by foreign and domestic investors alike.

---

crowded worker hostels, continuing to hold jobs where they may not even receive a salary, sustained by the hope that they might receive an apartment after their many years on waiting lists.[5]

---

[3] Evidence on real wages is from TACIS, *Moldovan Economic Trends, Quarterly Update* (February 1997). Data from the Moldova Household Budget Survey, 1997 are not well-suited to report on wage levels or trends.

[4] The 50 percent fall in real wages reported by the survey is subject to a number of qualifications, some of which suggest the decline may be overstated. First, any earnings received in-kind, especially housing, would mitigate the reported decline which only refers to that part of wages paid in cash. Second, enterprises have an incentive to under-report wages in order to avoid certain taxes such as the 35 percent tax to the Social Fund. Third, and working in the opposite direction, the enterprise surveys do not take account of those on forced/unpaid leaves. To the extent this number is rising, the decline in remuneration, averaged over both those who are employed and those who are on leave, could be higher. The changing skill mix of enterprises as a result of forced/unpaid leaves and separations would also affect the pattern of real wage changes reported by the survey.

The tendency to measure trends in household income through the trend in real earnings should, however, be avoided—given that it is a flawed indicator of true earnings in today's Moldovan economy. Official statistics of real earnings are a poor indicator of pay trends in smaller firms, including self-employment, that lie outside the official survey's sampling frame. Real wage trends in such activities may have increasing real wages for self-employed professionals and other occupations facing high demand, and stagnant or declining real pay for those engaged in petty trade and unskilled activities. Moreover, employment status, and wage and pension arrears are critical in measuring true incomes. Given rising unemployment and arrears in wage payments, some households may have experienced even more precipitous falls in real income. Alternatively, as households resort to survival strategies, earnings from secondary activities, including in-kind income from household plots (see Figure 2.7, page 33), offset the fall in enterprise earnings and cushion the blow of declining real wages.

Unemployment and poverty

Official unemployment figures grossly understate the number of unemployed, due to the behavior of both the workers and their employers. The majority of the unemployed in Moldova do not register as unemployed, since the meager benefits (mostly in arrears) of doing so do not outweigh the costs. Thus, calculating unemployment from household statistics (see Tool Box 2.3) yields a number—16.7 percent for 1997—that is far higher than official statistics.[6] For those on forced/unpaid leaves, registering as unemployed would cause them to lose any benefits—housing, medical, and so on—that they could receive by remaining nominally affiliated with an enterprise. Such workers also leave open the possibility of going back to work if the fortunes of their enterprises improve. In addition, there is the time and inconvenience associated with registering as unemployed, and a social stigma associated with being unemployed.[7] From the perspective of an enterprise, if workers are permanently laid-off, the firm is legally obligated to make

> **TOOL BOX 2.3: Estimating a seasonally-adjusted unemployment rate for Moldova**
>
> The household budget survey of February 1997 reports 9.7% of the adult population as "with a job but did not work," of whom 5.6% are engaged in agriculture. 4.1% are not engaged in agriculture and are assumed not to experience seasonal unemployment. For all others in this group, seasonal unemployment is assumed to last for one-third of the year, that is, for all unemployed workers normally engaged in agriculture. This adds 1.9% (one-third of 5.6%) to the seasonally adjusted estimate of unemployment.
>
> 5.9% of the adult population report "without a job but want to work". 57.7% are assumed engaged in agriculture -- the same percentage as in the "with a job but did not work" group -- yielding another 2.5% of the adult population attached to the non-agricultural sector and 3.4% unemployed in agriculture. For the latter group, seasonal adjustment (one-third of 3.4%) adds another 1.1% of the adult population to the estimate of annual open unemployment.
>
> Added together, 9.6% of the adult population are considered unemployed. In order to express an unemployment rate, it is necessary to determine the number of unemployed as a share of the labor force of working age. The labor force of working ages is 57.5% of the adult population, resulting in an estimate of seasonally-adjusted annual unemployment of 16.7%.

---

[5] de Soto and Dudwick (1997).

[6] Lindauer (1998).

[7] Moreover, not everyone is aware of the existence of an unemployment service, and even fewer make use of it. De Soto and Dudwick (1997) report that it takes 5-6 months to accumulate the necessary documents to register, the meager 18 lei per month compensation is paid with a delay of 3-4 months, and few jobs are offered in any case.

severance payments—a clear disincentive to fire workers. Thus, the prevalent form of labor shedding is forced or unpaid leave, much of which is equivalent to permanent lay-offs.

Within the labor force, the most vulnerable group are the underemployed, many of them on partial unpaid leave. These are those who are officially defined as employed (since they do some work) but work less than 30 hours a week. In February 1997, 31 percent of them were poor, compared with 23 percent for the economy as a whole. Fully-employed workers, who report over 30 hours during the past seven days, experience a considerably lower poverty rate of 18 percent.

The unemployed are also vulnerable, with 28 percent of them below the poverty line in February 1997. The unemployment number, in Indicator Box 2.4, is calculated from the household survey, and includes those individuals in the labor force who report working zero hours during the past seven days and indicate either having a job or wanting one. It is interesting to note that relatively few among the unemployed have primary education or below. But this should be understood in relationship to their small percentage in the labor force. While 18 percent of Moldova's adult population has a primary education or less, nine out of ten of them are out of the labor force, mostly because they are above official retirement ages. Overall, those with less than a secondary education constitute fewer than 5 percent of the labor force.

✓ **INDICATOR BOX 2.4: Who are the unemployed and why are they poor? (February 1997, including Transnistria)**

Attributes	Of the unemployed (%)	Unemploy-ment rate (%)	Poverty rate among unemployed (%)
Right Bank	94	30	28
Transnistria	6	11	54
Urban	32	20	29
Rural	68	33	31
Male	57	30	31
Female	43	24	29
Age 14-24	25	41	31
Age 25-50	69	26	29
Age over 50	6	14	35
University education	7	11	27
Vocational	26	21	23
Secondary	64	39	33
Primary/ illiterate	3	23	32

Source: Lindauer (1997).

Although there is considerable variation among the unemployed in terms of their attributes, there is relatively little variation in poverty rates within the group. Rural workers are significantly more likely to be unemployed (Indicator Box 2.4). Younger workers are more likely to experience unemployment than prime age adults and older workers. Those with only a secondary education make up two-thirds of the unemployed and have unemployment rates of 39 percent, well in excess of any other education group. However, poverty rates among the different categories of unemployed in Moldova had very little variance, falling within the narrow range of 27 to 33 percent. By way of an example, unemployment rates for someone with a university education are far less than those for someone with only secondary education. But once unemployed, poverty rates are similar for individuals with these two levels of education.

Therefore, unemployment, not the other characteristics, is key to poverty within these groups, and may be a significant explanation as to why these groups are over-represented among the poor. As analyzed in Chapter 1, young workers, those with only secondary schooling or lower and individuals who reside in rural areas are more likely to be poor. They are also, as seen in Indicator Box 2.4, more likely to be unemployed.

The lack of variance in poverty rates by attribute for the unemployed suggests that the returns to work activity are relatively flat, varying little according to individual attributes. For this reason, unemployed university graduates may not have significantly more resources to fall back upon than unemployed secondary school graduates. Once unemployed, both groups stand a similar chance of falling into poverty. This would be less likely in a fully market-oriented economy where those with less human capital would have a greater chance of falling into poverty because of an adverse event that results in unemployment.

Specific coping strategies: informal sector and seasonal migration

Entrepreneurial activities in the informal sector and seasonal labor migration to other countries have become critical coping strategies for households in Moldova. With both state and private sector formal employment less secure than in pre-independence times, and incomes from formal sector activities low and uncertain, such activities are the only way to ensure a fairly steady flow of incomes to the family. The environment for such activity is, however, highly risky, and thus adds to the average Moldovan household's uncertainty and anxieties about its income flows over the year.

Marketing crops from individual plots or gardens is an important way of generating income. As shown in Figure 2.7 (page 33) in the next section, this is a major income generator for landless workers in agriculture. For example, starting in November, people from Balti go by train to Odessa, taking 150-200 apples packed in cardboard boxes or in sacks—and sell them wholesale or at the market over 2-3 days. Alternatively, villagers may hire a bus and go to Ukraine or Russia, paying bribes up to $100 to customs officials. Another potentially more profitable way is to sell to middlemen from Russia, who drive their trucks directly to the villages and were paid, in 1997, about $1 per kilogram of apples. When the transactions are in barter terms, the reported rates are often extortionate: 8 kg of wheat for a bar of soap, 10 kg for a package of detergent, 200 kg for a pair of children's boots. [8]

VOICES: A 48 year old woman importer
"I do not know for how many more years I will be able to travel abroad [to Turkey and Poland] for merchandise. All these trips have damaged my health, and since I have no seniority at work, I cannot expect much from a pension. I am afraid to think about the future."
-- quoted in de Soto and Dudwick (1997)

Petty trade and small home-based enterprises have become an important support for many households. Marketing of goods and farm produce takes place within Moldova, as well as across borders with Romania, Ukraine, and other FSU and East European countries. Many use personal connections, access to resources, and skills or hobbies to start small home businesses, such as growing flowers and floral arrangements, carpentry, baking, knitting, and other crafts. People use kinship and other personal ties to find work or establishing "suitcase trading" relations, mostly with Turkey and Eastern European countries, but also throughout the FSU, and with Greece, Israel and Western Europe.

However, the lack of social capital is an obstacle, especially for the poorer entrepreneurs. To take enterprises beyond the level of unregistered micro-businesses to legitimate, mid-scale enterprises, Moldovans need both social capital ("contacts" or networks)

---

[8] This can also entail risks, as reported in de Soto and Dudwick (1997). In some reported cases, a police detained the loaded truck and driver. When they failed to reappear, the farmers realized that the police and middlemen had conspired to cheat them out of their payment.

and financial resources. Among the poorer members of society, the lack of a social network has proven to be a problem, especially as Moldovan society increasingly relies on patronage ties with the waning role of the state as employer and provider. Therefore, links with those who are well-placed, rich and powerful are critical for acquiring information, dealing with bureaucracy, and avoiding official harassment. Especially in rural areas, such relations play a central role, and local officials can easily restrict access to both information and resources.[9]

PERSPECTIVES: "Suitcase trade"

Marcu, a Moldovan, made money by using a loophole in customs regulations: Romania does not tax Moldovans who bring goods through their country. He teamed up with a Romanian partner, with whom he traveled to Turkey. There they bought goods which they resold in Romania. This earned him $200 a month.

Ira used to work as a secretary in the Ministry of Agriculture. She finally left the job because the salary was so low, and even then, paid with delays. On the advice of her sister, she borrowed $1,000 (without interest) from several relatives, and started importing goods from Poland. A typical trip involved the following expenses:

➢ $160 for bus transport and $20 in customs fees (paid to the bus driver, who assumed all risks related to "rackets.")

➢ 240 lei/month to rent a space in the market

➢ 100 lei/month for warehouse space

The best seasons were spring, and fall, just before school starts. In a good month, she made 400-500 lei; in a bad month, she only broke even.

--de Soto and Dudwick (1997)

Obtaining start-up capital also is a big problem for poorer people who wish to start small enterprises or private farming. In today's Moldova, banks rarely act as a true financial intermediary, since the costs of lending to individuals or small firms are exceedingly high. In the absence of widespread landholding, and a thin market for land resulting in an imperfect market pricing mechanism for land, collateralization is difficult. Moreover, the legal enforcement of contracts is not always possible or prompt. Most small entrepreneurs, therefore, borrow from neighbors, friends, and relatives. When they need larger amounts, they go to professional money-lenders to borrow at very high interest rates. This can have catastrophic consequences, especially when contract enforcement by the moneylenders is through harassment and intimidation, against which poorer households have no recourse.

As in other FSU countries, labor migration has become the quickest way to earn cash. Moldovans, with a stagnant labor market at home, have taken advantage of their location near the intersection of Europe and Asia, and their established migration patterns within the FSU, to move to markets with a higher demand for labor and higher remuneration. Migrants usually leave other family members back in Moldova, preferring to send money to them for their subsistence.

As shown in Figure 2.5, Moldova had a large exodus of people in the early 1990s—mostly to Russia and other FSU countries (230,000 people between 1990-95), but also to other countries, including Israel and Western Europe (about 60,000 people over the same period). Some of the early emigration, especially those to the other FSU countries, was for non-economic reasons, and the emigrants retained relatively little connections with Moldova. Later in the decade, however, the role of economic migration—especially temporary labor migration as "guest workers"—has become an important way for workers to support their families.

---

[9] de Soto and Dudwick (1997).

In 1996, approximately 11,000 Moldovan nationals were officially registered as working abroad, the majority in Russia. However, estimates of 15 times that amount have been made for the number of unregistered temporary migration in search of employment. Hard numbers are impossible to come by, but anecdotal and anthropological evidence supports this. Migrants travel to Russia, to Ukraine, Belarus, Hungary, to Romania (for trade), Greece (for agricultural work, housework, and child care), Germany, Israel and elsewhere. Rural inhabitants frequently leave their villages in autumn and winter, when there is less agricultural work to do. In Russia, the largest single destination, men work in heavy construction, or as builders and masons on private homes of the new rich, in agriculture on field brigades or as drivers and tractor operators.

The temporary emigrants, though primarily male, have increasing numbers of women joining their ranks. Both men and women travel to Russia, Ukraine, Romania, Greece and Hungary to work in agriculture. Women also travel to Turkey, Russia and elsewhere to market produce on the street or in produce markets, and work as small-scale street produce vendors in Turkey and Russia. Women in the Balti district travel in winter by train to Moscow to sell beans, nuts, garlic, and carrots in small quantities. Greece has become a significant destination for young women, who work as maids and nannies for $400-600 a month.

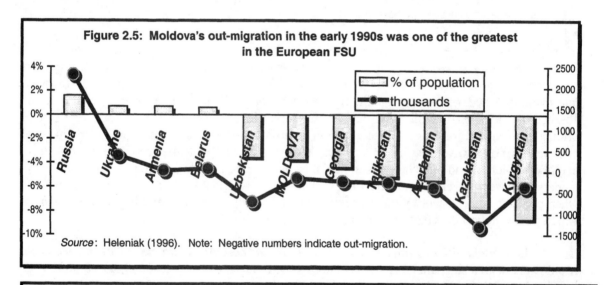

Figure 2.5: Moldova's out-migration in the early 1990s was one of the greatest in the European FSU

Source: Heleniak (1996). Note: Negative numbers indicate out-migration.

OVERALL POLICY MEASURES AND POVERTY

To reduce poverty across the board over the medium term, the only solution in Moldova is to create an environment where the market generates remunerative employment opportunities. Moldova, as a small open economy, is extremely vulnerable to external shocks. Thus, this is going to prove to be a difficult, though achievable, endeavor. Over the next few years, this will have to be done by extending the structural transformation of the economy to sectors beyond primary agriculture, to agro-processing, ancillary manufacturing, and an increase in the service sector. A critical element is going to be the building of channels for foreign trade and investment. Most important, Moldova's existing stock of human capital compared to GDP per capita is one of the highest in the world—and this advantage has to be maintained over the medium term and deepened over the longer term.

Agricultural employment and incomes

The biggest strides in poverty eradication over the medium run will have to come from resurgence in agriculture. As Comparator Box 2.5 shows, agriculture (including agro-processing) had almost half of all employment. As discussed earlier, poverty is concentrated among its landless wage workers. Only one in ten workers were in non-agricultural industry, and they were comparatively less poor. The number of the poor in agriculture is likely to decline as land is transferred, over the course of 1998 and 1999, away from old-style farming structures to individuals and households. Several key constraints remain, however, to a full-scale resurgence in agriculture that will significantly lift living

★ **COMPARATOR BOX 2.5: Moldova has one of the lowest share of workers in industry in the FSU (1996, percent of employed population)**

Country	Industry	Agriculture	Services
Tajikistan	8.9	59.5	27.8
Turkmenistan	9.8	43.8	37.2
Moldova	**10.3**	**46.1**	**40.0**
Kyrgyz Rep.	10.9	47.3	38.2
Azerbaijan	11.8	28.8	53.2
Uzbekistan	12.9	40.6	40.1
Kazakhstan	15.5	22.2	57.3
Armenia	18.6	38.0	38.6
Latvia	19.4	17.8	57.3
Lithuania	19.9	24.1	48.9
Estonia	22.9	7.2	57.6
Ukraine	23.5	22.2	48.2
Russia	25.4	14.4	51.1
Belarus	27.4	19.4	46.3

Note: Figures for Georgia were unavailable.
Source: Kuddo (1998).

standards of everyone in the agricultural sector. On the production side, the collapse of Soviet input and marketing monopolies have left vacuums in the production and marketing chains that are only gradually being filled by private agents. Credit remains a problem in an environment where the formal banking system finds lending to individual farmers risky and costly.

While incomes from agricultural activities are, and are likely to remain, the major source of income for large sections of Moldova's population, current working conditions imply that land ownership significantly affects incomes. This is demonstrated by the analysis in Chapter 1, where agricultural wage workers were one of the groups most at risk. "Farmers", however, who owned their own land, were much less likely to be poor. This section will explore the transformation occurring in Moldovan agriculture today, in an attempt to explain this phenomenon, and to lay the ground towards looking to the future of Moldova's largest group of the poor.

The restructuring of Moldova's farms that is now underway is aimed to provide individuals and families with the opportunity to have a larger role in determining their own income stream. As shown in

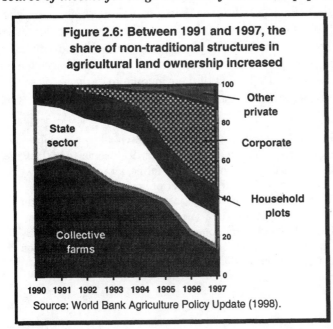

Figure 2.6: Between 1991 and 1997, the share of non-traditional structures in agricultural land ownership increased

Source: World Bank Agriculture Policy Update (1998).

Figure 2.6, land ownership in agriculture is undergoing rapid change—and the pace is picking up in 1999 and into 2000. The old state and collective farms, which together constituted over 92 percent of all agricultural land in Moldova in 1990, have given way to new forms of land ownership, including corporate structures (such as joint-stock companies), farmer's associations and peasant farms. By 1997, collective and state farms were just over 30 percent of agricultural land, while individual farms (including household plots) had grown to 21 percent of the total.[10]

While there are preliminary signs that true private farmers can significantly improve their incomes, some types of farm reorganization have not resulted in much improvement in the welfare of farm workers. In a 1996 survey of farm households, almost 40 percent of farm employees reported that their family income was insufficient for basic subsistence needs, while only 20 percent of private farmers were that pessimistic. This estimate is clearly subject to downward bias, but the comparison between the two groups is relevant. More significantly, three-quarters of the private farmers in the 1996 sample reported that their economic conditions had improved (or not gotten worse) since they became private farmers.[11]

As seen in Figure 2.6, (previous page) many collective farms have formally reorganized themselves into "joint stock companies", after the passage of the 1992 Law on Joint Stock Societies. However, in effect, there has been little change in their actual organization. While now the payments to workers consist of both salaries and "dividends" to use the workers' land shares, farm managers have retained their former role in the organization. Members are often treated essentially as wage workers, rather than participants with a say in decision-making. More troubling was the practice of inhibiting households from withdrawing land and non-land assets.[12]

VOICES: A young mother and farm worker
"When I go to the [farm] director, I don't know why, but I am afraid of him, I am afraid to talk to him. He never looks at you when you talk to him. He looks through the window, and then suddenly he screams 'What do you want? Go and work! I don't have any money!'"
--de Soto and Dudwick (1997)

Farm workers in Moldova usually have very little cash incomes from their wage labor. As Figure 2.7, from the 1996 survey of farm households shows, workers' incomes are dominated by in-kind payments, income from their own household plots, and other income (including pensions and "dividends"). After paying for their land and house taxes, and electricity charges, farm laborers, on average, are left with less than 15 percent of their income in cash. As is evident from the figure, they also are paid in produce, often valued at higher-than-market-rates.[13] Cash

---

[10] The process began soon after independence, with the distribution of small household plots and the 1992 adoption of the Land Code and the Law on Peasant Farms. By November 1994, some 14,000 families had withdrawn their land from collective farms to establish individual farms, and an additional 40,000-50,000 had submitted applications to do so. The large number of households wishing to privatize their land stirred opposition to land reform from conservative elements in the Moldovan polity, and led to the November 1994 Law on Suspension of Some Articles of the Land Code. In 1996, the Constitutional Court of Moldova declared restrictions on exit unconstitutional, and the process again accelerated. Currently, the "Land Program" of the Government is concentrating on breaking down old collective and State farms, and distributing land titles to the peasants.

[11] Lerman, Csaki and Moroz (1998).

[12] de Soto and Dudwick (1997).

[13] de Soto and Dudwick (1997) report payments such as: 1 leu per kg of potatoes, which could be purchased at the market for .80-90 lei, or sugar valued at 2.70 lei, but priced at 2.30 lei in the market.

wages, especially, are often in arrears for months, and adds to the hardships faced by farm workers.

The transformation going on in agriculture is not likely to improve incomes immediately, but is likely to do so over the medium term. Private ownership of land will improve the incentive to invest and to improve efficiency in the operation of the farm. It will also enable the farmers to keep a larger part of the surplus for themselves, rather than lose them to some of the more ineffective farm managers. But, for most new landowners, who have never been peasant entrepreneurs before, generating a sustained stream of income from farming is going to require the acquisition of new skills. A particular constraint, discussed more fully later in the chapter, is the availability of marketing and distribution channels for the products, especially local agro-processing facilities which can purchase products from the farmers and act as a conduit for exports of the processed commodities abroad.

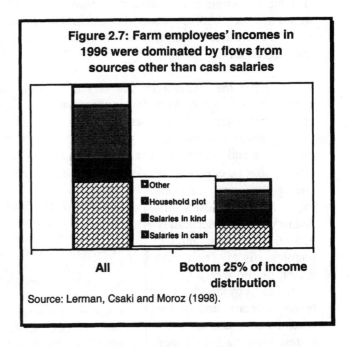

Figure 2.7: Farm employees' incomes in 1996 were dominated by flows from sources other than cash salaries

Legend: Other, Household plot, Salaries in kind, Salaries in cash

All / Bottom 25% of income distribution

Source: Lerman, Csaki and Moroz (1998).

A partial solution to these problems is the re-creation and expansion of Moldova's agro-processing industry. Moldova's produce is of excellent quality, but much of it is exported unprocessed—and thus its perishability limits the geographical reach of the country's exports. Much of existing agro-processing facilities are either outmoded and produce goods of a quality that is not competitive in the new international marketplace, or crumbling due to disuse and disrepair.[14] A capital injection, especially from foreign investors, would provide a needed boost to this sector. The revived agro-processors would provide seasonal credit and inputs to their suppliers, and in turn provide the suppliers with an easier market for their produce. To the extent that the owners of these agro-processing plants were based in Western Europe or other foreign countries, Moldova would also benefit by being able to use their marketing channels to export Moldovan processed agro-products to high-demand non-traditional markets. There is thus the possibility of larger surpluses in the agricultural sector, which, if reinvested by the farmers, would be able to drive the engine of its growth.

Within non-agricultural industry, what will be required is an increase in productive jobs, replacing currently unproductive industrial employment. The combined processes of job destruction and creation should lead to a turnover of jobs in the sector, but its overall share of total employment may be little changed. The restructuring of existing enterprises to their "viable core", which may involve changing their entire production lines to manufacture goods that are more in demand, is a key element in this process.

---

[14] An exception is the conglomerate INCON, which until a couple of years ago, was one of the largest exporters of apple juice concentrate in Europe. It has fallen on harder times, however, due to lower-priced competition from the Chinese.

As transition proceeds, Moldova's economy will follow the trend of countries in Central Europe, where employment will flow to the service sector. As agriculture becomes more efficient and competitive, there will clearly be a surplus of labor—which, over the longer term, would mean a labor flow out of the sector. Given that non-agro-processing industry is unlikely to be Moldova's area of longer-term comparative advantage, services are likely to be the recipient of this migration.

Over the longer term, poverty alleviation will be driven by a change in the mix of service sector activity from less remunerative to higher-paying occupations. Today, service sector employment is high (Comparator Box 2.5, page 31), reflecting almost a fifth of all workers in the health and education sectors, 10 percent in commerce (wholesale and retail trade, restaurants and hotels) and the remaining 15 percent spread among construction, transport and other public and private services.[15] Social sector workers, especially in education, are also among the poorer sections of society—most of primary and secondary education is public, and the ongoing fiscal crisis has driven public wages (when paid) at abysmally low levels. Construction, on the other hand, was one of the fastest growing (and hence well-paid) sectors in Moldova—with most activity being concentrated in and around Chisinau.

> **PERSPECTIVES: Enterprise restructuring**
>
> Many large enterprises have managed to change their production lines, and now work at quarter or less capacity. One such example is the former Lenin munitions plant in Balti, which employed 8,000 workers. Employment there was considered "prestigious," and it attracted many workers. Now it employs 2,000 workers to produce consumer items such as umbrellas, electric irons, toasters, and chandeliers, many of which remain in warehouses for lack of customers. Salaries have decreased from the once comfortable amount of 200-300 rubles to 100-150 lei, paid with a 2-3 month delay. In many cases, employees are forced to receive goods in kind, and must sell their supply of electric irons or toasters to local shops, or the market.
>
> -- de Soto and Dudwick (1997)

Trade, once again, is most active in Chisinau and other major urban centers—most of rural Moldova has yet to develop even the beginnings of a non-farm rural economy.[16] As transition proceeds and the economy itself recovers, the share of public employment is likely to fall in Moldova, driven by higher productivity occupations in emerging service sectors, especially in finance and trade. Higher-end services, dealing with trade- and enterprise-related finance activities, will gradually fill the breach.

---

[15] Estimates of employment include those on forced/unpaid leave.

[16] Most villages in Moldova are supplied by the local Mold-coop store. Mold-coop, essentially a trading monopoly in rural areas, operates throughout Moldova. Its unique supply chain and relatively low costs do not easily allow new traders to set up in competition.

TOOL BOX 2.6: Growth simulations

Only rapid growth in consumption will yield a large improvement in the welfare of the poor over the short run. What patterns of growth would yield the best results for Moldova? The answer is clearly growth that favors rural areas, and growth that improves inequality. It is an useful exercise to use the household survey data that exists in Moldova to simulate the results of different patterns of growth, to examine the policy options.

We consider two illustrative scenarios: a case of balanced growth, and inequality-reducing growth. *It should be noted that the simulations are not intended to be forecasts, but examples to demonstrate the effects of different growth patterns for Moldova.*

First, consider the scenario where everyone's consumption increases across the board at the optimistic average growth rate of 5 percent a year. In this stylized case, the absolute poverty headcount (the number of people consuming below the equivalent of 82.10 lei in May 1997) would fall from 46 percent in 1998 to 27.7 percent by 2004. The poverty headcount will drop to below 20 percent by the year 2008. If average growth rates are slower, the reduction of poverty to below 20 percent will take longer.

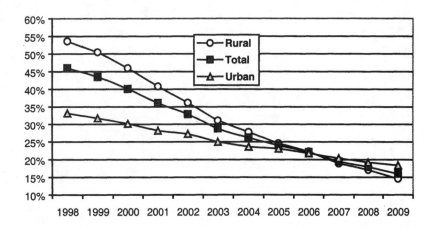

But, for such balanced growth, rural poverty (53.6 percent in 1998) would remain consistently higher than poverty in urban areas (33.2 percent in 1998). And the distribution of incomes will actually get worse, as the income disparity between rich and poor widens. Again, if growth is driven by economic activity concentrated mostly in Chisinau and other urban areas, either the overall increases in consumption will not result in corresponding decreases in poverty, or there will be increased migration from jobless rural areas to growing urban centers.

Agriculture-driven growth, however, has a chance of reversing this situation. Consider if this growth was driven by rising consumption in rural areas than urban (say, an average consumption growth of 6.5 percent in rural areas, versus 3 percent in urban, still giving us about 5 percent growth overall). Then, while overall rates of poverty reduction would be similar, rural poverty would decline faster, to drop below urban poverty rates (19 percent compared to 20.4 percent) by 2007.

Finally, what pattern of growth would improve Moldova's levels of inequality to those in Western European countries (i.e., around 0.3 as opposed to over 0.4 today)? Again, using the benchmark overall growth rate of 5 percent a year, this would happen within ten years if the consumption of the poorest grew much faster than those of the richest. In a simulation where the consumption of the poorest 40 percent grows at three times the rate of growth of the richest 20 percent, the Gini falls to 0.3 by 2009, comparable to the levels of inequality in France or Germany today.   Most strikingly, this also reduces poverty to a much greater extent compared to the other simulations: the poverty headcount in 2009, in this case, would be a mere 4.2 percent.

3. POVERTY AND THE ROLE OF THE STATE

In its efforts to directly alleviate poverty, the Moldovan Government has to overcome three mutually reinforcing challenges: the population's high expectations for broad and effective interventions, its own lack of fiscal resources, and the technical difficulties in finding effective targeting mechanisms for Moldova's shallow poverty. As a result of its lack of resources, the Government has both been a direct contributor to increasing poverty (through wage and pension arrears) and unable to assure essential services to the poor. Moreover, the Government's social protection system is ineffectively targeted, although social assistance payments have demonstrably pulled some Moldovan households out of poverty. In the near future, if the Government is to make an impact on poverty, it has to concentrate on consolidating its multiplicity of small benefits into a few larger, better targeted ones. These may include a set of self-targeted public works schemes that help alleviate poverty among the rural landless. Finally, Moldova may be venturing into an inter-generational poverty trap, as increasing numbers of poor children are dropping out of school, and poor families are failing to avail of health care services. Broad structural reforms in health and education will be needed to make public spending more efficient and directed towards the services most needed for the poor.

THE STATE AND POVERTY ALLEVIATION IN MOLDOVA

A key role of the Government in any society is to combat market failure—which includes the inability of purely private efforts to provide adequate sustenance for everyone in the population. The elderly, the disabled and children cannot (or, for children, should not) work. As we have seen from the analysis of Moldova's poor in Chapter 1, others in the economy may be employed, but unable to earn enough to sustain themselves and their family—the so-called "working poor". In each case, the Government has a role in helping to provide for their needs. Moreover, the Government's responsibility is not only to provide for the current well being of the population, but also to provide for their future welfare (through furnishing education and an environment conducive to employment generation).

> **VOICES: Several Moldovans**
> "It is the government's responsibility [to fix the situation]"
> —de Soto and Dudwick (1997)

This role clearly has to be balanced with the **ability** *of the Government to meet these needs, in terms of fiscal affordability and capacity to deliver services—and this is where Moldova faces a dilemma.* If the Government is not able, for whatever reason, to effectively combat the market failure of increased poverty, the result may be "government failure", even more ruinous for both the economy and the society. In Moldova, the Government faces three major problems in devising an effective poverty-alleviation policy:

> ➤ Poverty, as measured by societal experience and expectations, is pervasive: While grinding, absolute deprivation is rare, and food poverty isolated, most of the population has living standards that are low by European standards but, perhaps more important, are much lower than that which they enjoyed a decade ago. This is

compounded by the relative price shock, especially for energy, faced recently by Moldovan consumers.

➢ Due to the transformation in the economy, the Government is in fiscal crisis: With a prolonged economic recession exacerbated by the impact of the regional crisis in 1998, actual Government expenditures are unable to keep up with expenditure commitment patterns not fully adjusted for the change in Moldova's new economic structure and economic circumstances.

➢ Targeting expenditures narrowly to the most vulnerable groups is difficult, both technically and politically: Technically, much of Moldova's poverty is related to labor market outcomes and activities—and thus difficult to target in an environment where it is easy to conceal labor market activity and incomes. Moreover, given that poverty overall is both broad and shallow, technical targeting mechanisms such as Proxy Means Tests fail to effectively discriminate among Moldova's poor. Politically, it is difficult to remove entitlements from groups—such as pensioners, trade unions and the urban population—that have strong lobbies and move them to constituencies—such as children and the rural wage laborers—that are relatively without voice in Moldovan society.

As a result, the Government in Moldova is faced with an almost impossible situation of trying to provide a wide section of the population with benefits from a dwindling public purse. The obvious result, in Moldova, is that the Government fails in its efforts to mitigate the hardship of the population. It promises many people (including those who are clearly not poor) small amounts of various benefits, some of which relate to their poverty, and some of which do not. And because of its very limited finances, even these payments usually end up in arrears, alienating the population and worsening its political bind.

For the Government, the only escape from this vicious circle is to attempt, over the short run, to face the reality that it will have resources to target monetary benefits to the obviously poorest groups. Over the medium term, it has to move towards a system that allows it to have more flexibility in matching fiscal resources to the need for poverty alleviation. This has to be accompanied by attempts to protect the future of its population by ensuring that it has sufficient access to basic needs—basic health and, for its children, education—so that they have the ability, as the environment permits, to generate enough income to pull themselves out of poverty.

⎕ TOOL BOX 3.1: Strategies for poverty alleviation: different concepts

To devise an effective tool for combating poverty, it is critical for the Government to articulate its ultimate objective. Is it 'capabilities', incomes or welfare? (see van der Walle 1995) The first approach deals with how to provide people with capabilities--the means to avoid hunger, illiteracy or ill-health. Examples of such interventions are programs that improve basic education, and, in some cases, provide job re-training. The existence of an overall macro-growth environment that allows individuals to find well-paying jobs is consistent with this objective. The second is broader, and deals with mechanisms to provide income to people--to provide them with an increased ability to purchase goods and services. In addition to capabilities, this clearly includes direct income transfers. The third, and broadest, objective is to improve the welfare of people--providing them with not only more income but with other things that they may value, such as individual leisure or social equity. This is usually enabled through legislation that attempts to improve working conditions or access to resources (such as job quotas for the underprivileged).

While the differences between the three objectives are somewhat driven by a society's philosophy, they can also be driven more pragmatically by their affordability—the broader the objective, the more expensive it is going to be for society. In Moldova's case, the question for policymakers is whether its society is able to truly pay for the broadest approach to poverty alleviation.

This chapter examines the Moldovan Government's efforts at directly intervening to alleviate poverty in the economy. It begins with exploring the Government's resource constraint, and goes on to discuss its existing social protection system, and recommendations for its future design. It concludes with examining the Government's role in improving access to health and education for Moldova's poor.

The Government's resource constraint

Moldova's Government has been increasingly unable to meet its expenditure commitments, and the result has been a run-up of arrears. Moldova's transition economy, like others in the region, has seen a significant fall in revenue collections—as both the economy and tax compliance have shrunk. Concurrently, the need to stabilize the economy has put a cap on overall budgetary expenditures. Budgetary expenditures in the social sphere, including health and education, was 1,540 million lei (17 percent of GDP) in 1996, decreasing to about 1,430 million lei (14 percent of expected GDP) in 1997. At the same time, the Social Fund, which provides

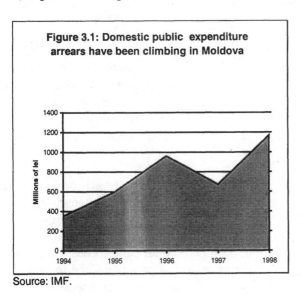

Figure 3.1: Domestic public expenditure arrears have been climbing in Moldova

Source: IMF.

pension and unemployment benefits primarily funded by the payroll tax, has seen a large drop in its cash collections, as enterprises have found themselves unable to generate enough revenues. But its expenditures have risen, from 766 million lei in 1996 to an expected 1,150 million lei in 1997. The worst off are the local governments, which have had to absorb some of the social services that were previously offered by enterprises in the regions, and also bear the burden of providing social services directly.

Public sector expenditure arrears, to public employees, pensioners and suppliers (especially suppliers of energy) have been mounting steadily since the mid-1990s (Figure 3.1), to reach 11.4 percent of GDP in end-1998, almost half of actual tax collections for the year. Over the past half-decade, the situation has worsened, due to a continued combination of overstated revenue targets, lack of provision for anticipated expenditure shocks and a lack of monitoring and control over local government spending, which have all essentially conspired to create a situation of "planned arrears".

Until last year, budgets were approved through a political bargaining process that preserved or expanded expenditure categories while relying on ambitious forecasts of increased revenues. These revenue increases seldom materialized, but expenditures did. However, especially for local governments, actual expenditures were often not in the categories that had been approved in the budget. Arrears were the result. Therefore, all levels of government in

---

VOICES: A pensioner
"If we only received pensions on time we could manage."
--de Soto and Dudwick (1997)

Moldova typically maintained their consumption through running up arrears—essentially by forced borrowing from pensioners, wage earners and input suppliers.

The Government has been moving to reduce its expenditure commitments, but has been hampered by a lack of a comprehensive program for the structural reform of expenditures, especially in the social sectors. Social sector expenditures, which are mainly the responsibility of local governments, have been cut across the board in an attempt to meet fiscal targets. However, in the absence of systematic restructuring of the sectors, all this has done is to force *ad hoc* cuts in real wages of service providers, ancillary inputs (such as medicines and school supplies) and repair and maintenance of facilities. At the same time, budgeted amounts have been unable to cover the cost of essential supplies, especially energy—with the result that these sectors have continued to accumulate expenditure arrears to their suppliers.

The Government's overall fiscal constraint has implied that many of the poor do not receive social services or transfers to which they are entitled. When the poor go to rural mayoralties, they often do not receive entitled payments on the grounds that the local government has not received any funds from the district budget. Some localities have dealt with this problem by giving out a form of "scrip"—in both Blesteni and Gordinesti, the Mayoralty distributed coupons which represented a certain sum, which families then redeemed for food at local shops.

However, there are large variations between rural and urban areas in how and when pensions and social payments are received. Chisinau, where economic activity has implied a more stable fiscal situation that in the rest of the economy, almost all pensions are paid on time and in full. In Balti, the second largest town on the Right Bank, pensions are received in late with delays of one or two weeks, while in nearby villages, villagers have not received their pensions in several months. In the poorer southern districts, pensions are received with several months delay Given that poverty is low in Chisinau, and lower in rural than in urban areas (Chapter 1), these delays exacerbate the geographical inequities.

The Government's fiscal problems have also made it unable to fully pay for its current transfers to the population. The Government adopted a poverty-alleviation strategy in 1998. However, the Government was unable to implement the strategy's recommendations for increased transfers to the poor, which were targeted relatively broadly. As shown in Indicator Box 3.2, its problems have led to a massive under-budgeting of the amount needed for the new transfers it has instituted over the last two years to compensate the population for increases in energy prices (the transfer programs themselves are discussed in detail in the next section).

Over the next year and further, the Government is attempting to construct a realistic budget that focuses expenditures only on priority areas while increasing the efficiency of its spending. This will allow it to reduce the spread of its social expenditures and transfer, but

✓ **INDICATOR BOX 3.2: The Government has been unable to budget enough to fully pay for legislated energy price compensations**

(thousand lei)	1998 total cost	1998 budgeted	1998 paid	1999 total cost	1999 budgeted
Electricity	93,335	50,000	47,487	104,516	50,000
Gas	10,000	10,000	2,342		
Heating	110,000	106,000	106,000	268,000	150,000
Total	213,335	166,000	155,829	372,516	200,000

Source: Sandu (1999)

ensure that those who deserve them most receive sufficient amounts in a timely and non-discriminatory fashion.

SOCIAL PROTECTION AND SOCIAL SERVICES

Moldova inherited a social protection philosophy and system from the former Soviet Union which has proved to be unsuited for the immediate needs of the transition itself, much less the requirements of a modern market economy. ***Pensions remain the major government transfer to the population, with small social assistance schemes such as child benefits and social pensions—being added on a sporadic basis.*** The entire system of social insurance (sick pay, maternity benefits, and pensions) was essentially linked to formal employment, which, together with fringe benefits and price controls, were supposed to provide for all the workers' needs. Maternity leave, sick leave, university study and special work-release retraining educational programs, as well as military service all were counted into the worker's *stazh* (work-tenure).

This left only "social parasites" such as criminals or invalids, who were unable to work regularly, as the primary concern of the social protection system. ***Given that there are now a large number of "working poor" in Moldova, the existing pension-dominated system is inadequate to meet the needs of all the poor.*** This is despite an array of benefits, including age-related pensions (paid according to age, even though person could still be working), old-age pensions (paid according to period of service and difficulty of work), disability pensions, pensions paid to dependents of deceased person, and social pensions. There are also other social benefits, including unemployment benefits, allowances for families with many children, and social insurance benefits. And, as a legacy from the Soviet times, there is an array of privileges or *l'goty*, which provide discounted services to a wide range of the population.

✓ **INDICATOR BOX 3.3: Privileges in Moldova are extensive and expensive (1998 data)**

CATEGORY	BENE-FICIARIES	TOTAL BENEFITS (THOU. LEI PER YEAR)	AVERAGE BENEFITS (LEI PER MONTH)
PENSIONERS	**685,230**	**338.7**	**41**
With more than 3 minimum pensions	211,230	91.0	36
With less than 3 minimum pensions	474,000	247.7	44
DISABLED	**118,116**	**202.1**	**143**
Group I	16,300	49.0	250
Group II	73,800	113.2	128
Group III	16,050	10.3	54
Families with disabled children	9,800	27.3	232
Disabled families with children	2,166	2.3	90
WAR-RELATED BENEFITS	**136,500**	**158.3**	**97**
War participants	45,000	70.9	131
War disabled	13,000	30.1	193
Spouses/children of those who died on duty	8,850	15.1	142
Civil war participants	60,000	33.5	47
Children of civil war participants	250	0.1	40
Prisoners of concentration camps	600	0.8	117
Spouses of war dead	2,800	0.8	23
Persons with medals	5,800	6.7	96
Medals for defense of Leningrad	200	0.3	110
STUDENTS	**235,747**	**55.0**	**19**
PROFESSIONAL CATEGORIES	**73,357**	**57.5**	**65**
Rural health/education workers	33,290	20.0	50
Police officers	20,575	28.4	115
Deputies and counselors	6,723	5.0	62
Lawyers & prosecutors	353	0.2	47
Pediatricians & nurses	6,816	0.7	8
Bus drivers	5,600	3.2	48
CHERNOBYL	**6,949**	**3.0**	**36**
Affected by Chernobyl	214	0.3	117
Families of Chernobyl victims	75	0.0	27
Chernobyl liquidators	3,300	2.5	63
Children born after Chernobyl	3,360	0.2	50
TOTAL	**1,263,329**	**817.5**	**54**

Source: Ministry of Finance, IMF estimates.

> **VOICES: Collective farm worker, Cahul district**
> If assistance for people from different social groups ever comes at all, no one ever knows what happens to it -- there is anarchy in our village, and I wouldn't even like to talk about this.
> --de Soto and Dudwick (1997)

Privileges and compensations

Moldova, like many FSU countries, has a broad array of special privileges for specific categories of people deemed to be worthy of receiving transfers (not necessarily needy). These special privileges are the provision of no-cost or low-cost food and consumer goods and services, especially fuel such as coal, and reduced fares for inter- and intra-city transportation. Along with the rest of the FSU, Moldova in general and sometimes specific localities, adopted these privileges in an *ad hoc* and unorganized way. Indicator Box 3.3 on the previous page attempts to enumerate them to the best of the Government's knowledge as of mid-1998.

In Moldova, privileges are given to six groups of individuals: pensioners, students, the disabled, war veterans and their families, members of certain professions, and a small group of people affected by the Chernobyl disaster. Overall, almost 1.3 million Moldovans (well over a third of the population of the Right Bank) enjoy these privileges. There has been some movement towards reducing the number of these privileges, however. The 1999 Budget Law cancelled privileges for police and prison workers, firemen, jurists, Chernobyl liquidators and the families of Chernobyl victims, and victims of political repression. As can be seen from Indicator Box 3.3 , however, many more remain, and would need to be eliminated over time to reduce the expense to the economy.

Privileges, depending on the beneficiary, can be benefiting either the poorer sections of society or the non-poor. The key, however, is that few of them were instituted as pro-poor measures—instead, they were rewards given to certain sections of the population that the Soviet society wanted to recognize and subsidize. Therefore, from a poverty alleviation standpoint, while discounted energy payments to Group I (completely) disabled individuals, families with many children, and rural health and education workers seem reasonable, it is less easy to justify privileges going to lawyers, the richer pensioners, or bus drivers.

✔ **INDICATOR BOX 3.4: The Government has been unable to budget enough to compensate energy enterprises for the privileges they are providing to the population**

(thousand lei)	1998 total cost	1998 budgeted	1998 paid	1999 total cost	1999 budgeted
Electricity	49, 985	2,058	2,034	30,775	0
Gas	30,000	1,846	2,817	19,400	0
Heating	27,000	0	0	38,600	0
Total	148,851	3,904	103,081	130,641	0

Source: Sandu (1999).

The system is extremely expensive for the economy as a whole, and particularly for the enterprise supplying the privilege. In 1998, privileges cost the economy over 800 million lei (around 8 percent of GDP). Privileges are essentially an implicit subsidy provided by an enterprise. Technically, the Government is supposed to compensate the enterprise for this subsidy. The mechanism for this compensation is, however, complex, and the Government has in recent years simply not budgeted enough to pay for the privileges. Indicator Box 3.4, which mirrors Indicator Box 3.2 (page 40) on compensations, shows the situation for energy-related privileges for 1998 and 1999.

Clearly, the Government, by not budgeting for the privileges, is passing on an enormous expenditure burden to enterprises—especially the energy enterprises. In 1998, of the estimated 149 million lei in energy-related privileges, the Government only paid for less than 4 million lei, leaving the burden of the subsidy on energy companies. In 1999, it has not even included the small amount that was in the 1998 budget.

In any case, it is doubtful whether the system as a whole is helping poverty. The reason is that, while individuals (some of whom are poor) are helped by the fact that the privileges cushion their relative price shock, the economy as a whole has enormous leakages from the system to the non-poor. Privileged consumers of electricity have a much higher consumption level than regular customers—during the first half of 1998, the average monthly consumption of privileged consumers was 332 kWh[1], versus 100 kWh for the rest of population. Moreover, the mounting losses of the energy companies, part of which are due to the privileges, have added greatly to Moldova's external debt, and the resultant debt service, in turn, has squeezed the Government's budget—making it difficult for it to afford more pro-poor intervention measures. Privileges, therefore, are clearly a sub-optimal method for poverty eradication, and need to be replaced with more direct and transparent methods to reach the poorest.

One such major poverty-related transfer program instituted in 1997 was a system of "compensations" for energy price increases. These transfers were instituted with some attention given to narrow targeting, with the compensations given to people with incomes of 150 lei a month or below. The income certification process, however, is problematic, as there is no way of determining true household incomes of beneficiaries—merely the official income from wages (which are usually understated by employers to avoid the payroll tax) or Government transfers. Thus, there may be large leakages to the non-deserving. However, as seen in Indicator Box 3.2, the Government is unable to pay all of these compensations, and thus is unable to fully meet its objective.

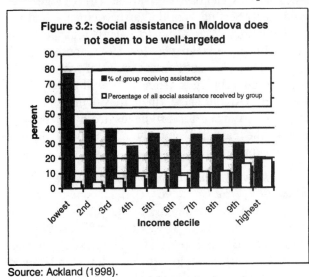

Figure 3.2: Social assistance in Moldova does not seem to be well-targeted

■ % of group receiving assistance
□ Percentage of all social assistance received by group

percent

Income decile: lowest, 2nd, 3rd, 4th, 5th, 6th, 7th, 8th, 9th, highest

Source: Ackland (1998).

In late 1998, the Government instituted a different method to provide compensations for increases in prices for district heating—a "lifeline" system based on the area of the apartment heated. The first 9 m[2] per person of *all* heated apartments received heat at an almost 80 percent discount. While this system is only targeted very broadly, by making residents of larger apartments (who are presumed to be richer) pay more, it effectively provides an element of subsidy to the entire population, and thus cannot be considered pro-poor at all. To make things worse, since consumption is measured by the floor area of the apartment, there are no associated benefits from decreased consumption in order to get under the lifeline. This system is also extremely expensive for the Government, and therefore

---

[1] Sandu (1999).

needs to be replaced by a system that subsidizes only the vulnerable groups in the population, and only up to a certain level.

The Government, in 1999, has begun taking major steps to rationalize its privileges and compensation strategy. This is being done in parallel with reform of the energy sector, as a forerunner to restructuring and privatization of the power, gas and district heating companies. The Government has a four-tiered strategy in this area: (a) remove the communal services compensation scheme, which is poorly targeted, and unaffordable for the budget; (b) eliminate all energy and transportation privileges issued by either Government resolution, Presidential decree, or by law; (c) install in its place an interim energy compensation scheme targeted to specific categories of the population which are deemed to be most in need of social assistance, and ensure that payments are made in full and in cash to the beneficiaries (as opposed to only partially and to the energy enterprises); and (d) develop a comprehensive social assistance strategy for the medium to long term which eliminates all privileges, while putting in place an effectively targeted social assistance program that is tied in magnitude to the envelop of budget revenues in any given year.

In June 1999, the Government took the first bold steps by eliminating the communal services compensation scheme and all energy and transportation privileges which had been issued by Government resolution. The Government also adopted draft Presidential decrees and draft laws which would remove the rest of the energy and transportation privileges, and replace them with one compensation scheme for communal services[2], mandated by law, for four categories of Moldovan citizens: (i) Category I invalids; (ii) Category II invalids; (iii) Second World War participants; and iv) invalid children. According to calculations provided by the Ministry of Finance for 1999, these actions would reduce the entitlement cost of energy and transportation privileges from 127 million lei to 47 million lei. At the same time, they will require an increase in payment for privileges from the budget, which in the past had actually not been paying for privileged entitlements.

✓ **INDICATOR BOX 3.5: Social assistance does play a role in pulling some households out of poverty in Moldova**

	Non-poor	Poor
Social Assistance		
ex post	39.6	29.7
ex ante	31.5	56.7
Pensions		
ex post	37.7	27.9
ex ante	29.8	54.8
Other Social Benefits		
ex post	2.9	2.2
ex ante	2.5	4.0

Notes: ex post: household incidence of receipt of benefit where poverty status is determined using total household consumption; ex ante: household incidence of benefit where poverty status is determined using total household consumption less amount of benefit received. Source: Ackland (1998): May 1997 data.

These actions are only the first steps toward rationalizing the system. The energy-related privileges and compensations accounted for less than half of the total cost in 1998 of over 800 million lei (see Indicator Box 3.3, page 41). The next urgent step is for the Government to eliminate all privileges, and replace them with an affordable targeted social assistance program. Toward this end, the Government is working to develop an action plan to be implemented as a part of the Public Sector Reform agenda during the year 2000.

---

[2] The scheme covers: (a) public utilities (heating, gas, cold and hot water, lift, trash haulage, and sewerage); (b) electricity; (c) natural gas used for heating; and (d) coal and firewood. Implicitly, transportation privileges are removed.

Targeting of existing benefits

Although the very poorest in Moldovan society are well covered by social assistance, a considerable amount of it "leaks" to higher income groups. This can be seen in Figure 3.2, where the darker bars represent the percentage of each income decile receiving pensions or other social assistance benefits in May 1997. The poorest 10 percent of the population are reasonably well-covered by social assistance, with over three-quarters of them benefiting. However, there is much less variance among other income groups, with 30 to 40 percent of individuals in the second to the ninth decile receiving benefits, and one-fifth of the richest 10 percent get benefits. The lighter bars show a more telling statistic. Representing the percentage of all social assistance received by the income group, it shows that the richest 10 percent of the population actually enjoys almost a fifth of all social assistance payments, while poor households received only 8.2 percent of allocated transfers. This pattern of receipt of benefits was very similar to that found for pensions (where poor households received 8.3 percent). This demonstrates that while the poor do receive some amount of benefits, these are very small in absolute terms, and the small number of the rich receiving benefits get relatively large amounts. In fact, the May 1997 data shows that 57.6 percent of non-poor households received social assistance—a significant leakage rate. At the same time, fully 38 percent of poor households got no form of social assistance at all.

The targeting of other social benefits (unemployment benefits, allowances for families with many children, and social insurance benefits) appears to be even less pro-poor. Poor households received 4.6 percent of the total amount of other social benefits allocated. The apparent poor targeting of unemployment benefits and social insurance benefits is not surprising, since these are linked to employment. As discussed in Chapter 2, many of the poor are unemployed. Again, while multi-child benefits are pro-poor in theory, anecdotal evidence suggests that this benefit has simply not been paid recently in some areas in Moldova.

On the other hand, social assistance transfers in Moldova do seem to have a significant effect in pulling households out of poverty. Indicator Boxes 3.5 and 3.6 look at two different definitions of poverty of a household in Moldova: *ex post*, which is the effective definition we have been using so far in this report, and *ex ante,* looking at their poverty status if they had not received social assistance benefits. In Box 3.5, if we look *ex post* at who among Moldovan households were receiving social assistance, only 29.7 percent of the poor households were beneficiaries. On the other hand, 56.7 percent of *ex ante* poor households received social assistance. If these households were consuming the entire amount of the social assistance, then social assistance in Moldova does move some households out of poverty. A similar story also holds for the incidence of receipt of pensions and other social benefits for poor and non-poor households. The incidence of receipt of both pensions and other benefits is higher for non-poor households when the *ex post* living standards measure is used—but the incidence for poor households approximately doubles when the *ex ante* welfare measure is used.

Poverty in Moldova is fairly shallow in that there are many households clustered just below the poverty line. Thus, targeted benefits are effective in moving households out of poverty. This can be seen from Box 3.6, which shows the impact of targeting on different poverty

---

✓ **INDICATOR BOX 3.6: Social assistance targeting can lower poverty in Moldova**

Consumption measure	Head-count	Poverty Gap
Ex post	19.0	6.2
Ex ante (social assistance)	27.1	11.8
Ex ante (pensions)	26.5	11.7
Ex ante (other social benefits)	19.5	6.3

Notes: ex post: poverty index using total household consumption; ex ante: poverty index using total household consumption less amount of benefit received.
Source: Ackland (1998): May 1997 data.

measures. Without social assistance and pension transfers, poverty would have been about 8 percent higher in each case, and the poverty gap would have been five and a half percent higher as well. Other social benefits, as before, do not seem to make much of a difference. This is an important policy conclusion—but the challenge is to find effective mechanisms to target the poor.

Toward an affordable and effective social protection system

As discussed at the beginning of the chapter, *the Government must try and match its resources and ability to address poverty with its desire to do so.* Over the medium term, it is unlikely that Moldova will generate sufficient resources to establish an income transfer system that has enough funds to be the most effective way to lift poor Moldovans out of poverty. One way to try and estimate the amount of fiscal resources necessary to do this is to consider the size of the total poverty gap *ex ante*, prior to social spending. From Indicator Box 3.6, this is of the order of 12 percent of consumption—an impossibly high barrier for Moldova at its current stage of economic transition and development.

Principles to guide Moldova's social protection philosophy

➢ *The generation of sufficient fiscal resources* through the elimination or drastic reduction of transfers that are either wasteful or badly targeted to the poor. This includes privileges, and some categories of social assistance benefits. This needs to be accompanied by an examination of the existing system of social protection, in order to clearly determine the rationale and utility of each of the multitude of overlapping benefits.

➢ As resources (or donor funds) permit, *the creation of "self-targeted" assistance programs* to help the poor (especially in rural areas) weather sudden economic shocks.

➢ *Over the medium term, a move towards the creation of a comprehensive targeting mechanism* that would allow an expansion of the social safety net to cover more people as Government's resources expand.

Thus, any reform in the system of social assistance in Moldova has to be built on increased access to the poor, and cost-effectiveness. The reform will have to acknowledge that the traditional groups receiving social assistance may only comprise a small part of those most in need—and many of these groups may be less vulnerable, and thus less in need of protection, than others. Concurrently, enhanced social assistance to the poorest will have to be in a system that is flexible and affordable, so that the Government is not trapped into promising a strategy that creates entitlements that it cannot deliver. Since current resources are very restricted, they should be narrowly spent to bring about the greatest improvements in the living standards for the poorest. As the resources of the Government increase, the social assistance mechanism could also expand, so that the Government is able to help provide a better standard of living to more of the population. However, creating an entitlement system by, for example, legislating that all individuals are entitled to a certain percentage of an arbitrarily determined "minimum existence level" could prove to be disastrous, since the resulting transfer system would have no link to the resources actually available to the Government.

The analysis in this report points to some particular areas where the Government can most effectively intervene in poverty alleviation.

PERSPECTIVES: The perception of poverty in Britain
In the 1930s, working families were seen as the main group in poverty: the main causes being unemployment and low earnings among men with large families. By the 1950s and 1960s, pensioners were the major cause for concern. Now the position has changed again, and in 1985, it is families with children who face the most difficult problems.
--Department of Health and Social Security, United Kingdom, 1985 "Reform of Social Security", p. 2, quoted in Atkinson (1995).

An essential first step is the creation of sufficient fiscal breathing room to allow resources for pro-poor programs. With Moldova's current fiscal crisis, it is difficult (if not impossible) for the Government to concentrate on devising an approach to poverty alleviation that is robust over the medium term. In today's Moldova, there is a vicious cycle of initiatives created in response to short-term demands that are under-funded—and thus end up not helping the poor – which again creates political pressure for new social programs. A first step towards breaking this cycle is to move towards remedies that simultaneously free up resources and do not hurt the poorest. Moldova is already undertaking a thorough and far-sighted reform of its pay-as-you-go pension system, which will help in this process over the next decade. Over the short run, the elimination of privileges is a first step, and the improved targeting of the compensation for heat is a necessary second step. Finally, the least costly and most progressive step in this direction is to improve tax collection from the small group of the very rich in Moldova, who escape virtually unscathed through the revenue net.

Any new transfers would need to be in cash and be sufficient to make a difference. As discussed in Chapter 1, one of the most evident aspects of poverty in Moldova is the shortage of cash to buy non-food consumables. Any transfer would, however, need to be large enough in absolute terms to make a difference in the recipient's purchasing power and be cost-effective for the Government. For example, benefits of 8 lei a month (the average privilege enjoyed by a pediatrician or nurse) are welcome to the recipients, but will hardly affect their poverty status. On the other hand, they carry a large administrative cost, and the total cost for such benefits, when given across the board to many individuals, can be significant. The privilege to nurses and pediatricians, for instance, costs the economy 700,000 lei every year—an amount that, if spread over a smaller number of the very poor, could make a significant difference in their lives.

PERSPECTIVES: Discretionary aid to the poor

In all [appeals for help to authorities], personal relations "have a strong word to say." Thus, the former chairman of a collective farm in the Comrat district receives free supplies of fire wood, coal, and 200 kg of straw as forage for his animals.

--de Soto and Dudwick (1997)

Narrow targeting of benefits presents a problem in Moldova. Income-based targeting, of course, is inadvisable in an economy where the institutional structure is too weak to support true verification of family incomes. the presence of a large informal sector makes it both difficult and administratively costly to accurately estimate household income. In countries such as Moldova, where many households rely on produce grown in private garden plots, the task of estimating household welfare is even more difficult; imputing the value of home-produced goods requires detailed information on exactly what produce was consumed by the household and market prices with which to value this consumption.

It is also difficult to easily discriminate among the population on the basis of easily verifiable indicators. "Proxy means tests" (Tool Box 3.7) have been used relatively successfully in other parts of the FSU to find indicators that are highly correlated with poverty. But such tests carried out with household data for both February and May 1997 were not able to predict poor households in Moldova with any degree of accuracy. This may be partly caused by problems of data, and thus there is a possibility that as the quality of the data improves, this can become a more useful policy tool.

TOOL BOX 3.7: Proxy means tests for Moldova

A major difficulty with administering a social assistance program is the accurate identification of eligible households. A proxy means test is a method of identifying the poor using household information which is reasonably easy and cheap to collect. The method involves using regression techniques to estimate a consumption function, and including several easily verifiable variables: wage income, public-transfer income, and dummy variables reflecting durable ownership and the presence of different household amenities. The coefficients from the consumption function are then used to predict household welfare and to calculate how many households are correctly predicted poor. If the model is reasonably good at identifying the poor, then it may be used as input into a social assistance targeting procedure which uses easily identifiable indicators (the eligibility of households for social assistance will depend on their predicted consumption as calculated using the estimated coefficients from the regression).

In analysis with May 1997 data, Ackland (1998) found that while the regressions were very good at predicting the poverty status of non-poor households (over 98 percent of the non-poor are correctly identified), they were less successful at identifying poor households. In the Right Bank, only 3.6 percent of those households known to be poor (based on actual household consumption) were predicted as being poor. These results confirm the equally disappointing findings by Braithwaite (1997) with February data.

The results of proxy means testing in other FSU countries have been more encouraging; more than 50 percent of poor households were correctly identified using proxy means tests in Estonia, the Kyrgyz Republic and Russia. Unfortunately, it appears that the prediction success rates are not high enough for proxy means tests to be used as input into social assistance targeting in Moldova.

The best option for targeting benefits in Moldova, therefore, is to use transfers using broad-based categorical indicators that are highly correlated with poverty. These may include cash transfers only to the worst-off among the disabled, to the elderly poor, especially those living alone or those not covered by the minimum pension guarantee. Another choice, that would help more vulnerable families, would be a single parent allowance for large families. To be even more effectively targeted, correlates could be combined—for example, disabled pensioners, or families of rural landless laborers. The proposed 1999 system of targeting privileges to invalid children is a good example of focusing on the intersection of two vulnerable groups. An effective intervention of this kind could go a long way towards easing some of the most egregious poverty.

In the absence of fully satisfactory ways to target using categorical indicators, public works programs that use "self-targeting" could be devised as a supplementary anti-poverty measure. Such programs do not let administrators decide who is eligible—instead, they create incentives that ensure that only the poor will avail of them. Given Moldova's high rural poverty rate, and the pattern of weather-related shocks that frequently lower agricultural incomes, the institution of a public works mechanism (Tool Box 3.8) would be appealing. Such a program, which would have a work requirement and relatively low wages for the work, would only benefit the poor, given that the opportunity cost for the better off would be too high for them to want to avail of such work. The program would also be elastic, expanding to absorb more poor people if incomes drop due to a systematic shock, and then contracting in better times. However, the unpredictability of the fiscal cost of such a program suggests that Moldova may want to seek donor partnerships in order to design and fund it.

TOOL BOX 3.8: Elements of a good self-targeted "workfare" program

"Workfare" programs attempt to reduce poverty by providing low-paid work to those who need it. They are flexible, in the sense that as the labor market improves, the demand for such work, and thus the cost, falls. But for such programs to be effective, Ravallion (1999) suggests that they have to be designed with some essentials in mind:

➢ Wage rates should be below market wages for unskilled manual labor in agriculture or the informal sector wage, so that people do not leave existing work to avail of higher-paid public employment;

➢ If fiscal constraints mean that more people are likely to apply than can be funded, the program should be focused on just the poorest areas (e.g., rural areas with limited agricultural reform);

➢ The actual work done should be more labor intensive than in similar projects in the area;

➢ The assets created should be chosen to be of most benefit to the poor; if they benefit the non-poor, the beneficiary group should share in the cost, with the funds going back to the workfare program.

TOOL BOX 3.9: Building a flexible targeted scheme: Armenia's PAROS

For distributing limited foreign humanitarian assistance so that it reaches those most in need, Armenia has used a system that ranks households according to a weighted average of different poverty characteristics. These characteristics include declared income, but also more easily validated attributes like location, refugee status, handicap and family size. Each attribute has an associated point value. For a household, a weighted average of the points for family members is calculated. Then all households are ranked according to their points, from the poorest to the richest. Finally, the resources available are distributed beginning with the poorest families. The system has the advantage of being flexible, since it can expand to cover more families as resources increase. At the same time, those most in need are always covered. This system, named PAROS, is now being refined, for use for a wider range of social assistance.

Over the medium term, Moldova should think about moving to a system that combines categorical targeting with fiscal flexibility. Such a system would provide cash benefits to just the poorest in society; however, the cut-off level for the benefit would depend on the Government's own resources. A system such as that of Armenia (Tool Box 3.9) could be a model for such an approach.

The most difficult element of moving to a scheme targeted to the poor in a fiscally constrained environment such as Moldova is the fact that putting such programs in place necessarily involve removing others that are badly targeted, but benefit politically important groups.[3] But there, a well-designed program can help ease some of these political obstacles. One tested way is to define the costs of the existing, expensive program in terms of tradeoffs for schools, hospital beds, and lost jobs.[4] People are also more tolerant of new programs which favor work requirements, since they believe that this would not be accessed by the undeserving. Building coalitions and participation in the design process of wide-ranging groups, such as farmers' associations and community activists—and an associated public information campaign--can also help.

---

[3] This problem is common to all countries, including the US and European nations, where universal programs such as social security and Medicare are supported much more than aid targeted to needy families (van der Walle 1998).

[4] Such as that done for the reform of an universal food subsidy to a targeted scheme in Tunisia (Tuck and Lindert 1996).

IMPROVING ACCESS TO HUMAN CAPITAL FOR THE POOR

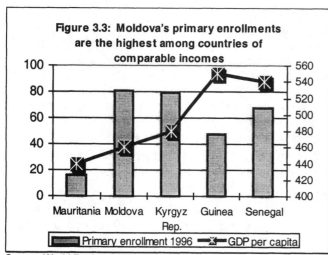

Figure 3.3: Moldova's primary enrollments are the highest among countries of comparable incomes

Primary enrollment 1996 — GDP per capita

Source: World Bank data.

Access to education

Moldova has one of the highest endowments of human capital for a country at its level of income. With a 1997 per capita income of US$460, it ranked alongside countries such as Mauritania (US$440), Kyrgyz Republic (US$480), Guinea (US$550) and Senegal (US$540). However, with a 97 percent enrollment rate in primary school, and a 26 percent enrollment rate in tertiary education, it far outstripped most of its peers in terms of participation in education and educational outcomes (Figure 3.3). This is despite its relatively low educational attainment when compared to other Soviet republics (Comparator Box 3.10).

There has, however, been a sharp contraction in Government expenditures on education, which has caused the relative quality of education accessed by the poor to fall. Public expenditures on education has fallen from 7.5 percent of GDP in 1994 to just over 6 percent in 1998. Better-off households have attempted to offset this by utilizing more private education. Thus, there is an increasing divergence in both quantity and quality of education received by poor and non-poor households.

★ **COMPARATOR BOX 3.10: Before independence, Moldova had relatively low educational attainment among Soviet republics**

Country	% of population 15 or older who completed or had incomplete	
(1989)	HIGHER Education	SECONDARY Education
Tajikistan	8.9	11.0
Turkmenistan	9.7	13.5
Moldova	**10.0**	**15.1**
Kyrgyz Rep.	11.0	15.7
Uzbekistan	11.1	15.0
Kazakhstan	11.7	18.5
Ukraine	11.9	18.0
Belarus	12.3	16.9
Lithuania	12.4	19.4
Azerbaijan	12.5	14.4
Russia	13.0	19.2
Estonia	13.5	19.6
Latvia	13.8	16.8
Armenia	16.1	17.9
Georgia	17.5	18.7

Source: GOSKOMSTAT, cited by Kuddo (1998).

Enrollment rates for the poor are lower in Moldova than for the non-poor, especially in Chisinau. Indicator Box 3.11 shows enrollment rates for children aged 6-16 years. The general enrollment rate of non-poor children is around 5 percentage points higher than their poor counterparts. This can be traced to the enrollment situation in urban areas (enrollment rates for the non-poor are only slightly higher in rural areas). In Chisinau, enrollment rates of poor children are over 20 percentage points lower than those of non-poor children, and in other cities in the Right Bank this difference is around 12 percentage points.

✓ **INDICATOR BOX 3.11: The poor access education less**

	Poor	Non-poor	Total
Chisinau	65.7*	87.1	84.6
Other cities	83.6	95.7	92.5
Rural			
male	89.4	89.3	89.3
female	84.2	89.7	87.9
all	87.0	89.5	88.7
Total			
male	86.3	90.3	89.1
female	83.5	90.4	88.5
all	85.1	90.3	88.8

Note: Asterisk denotes cell size less than 20; estimates may be unreliable.
Source: Ackland (1997), from Moldova Pilot Survey Data, February 1997.

One of the reasons for the difference in general enrolment rates between poor and non-poor children is differential rates of pre-school enrolment. Children aged less than 7 years are eligible for pre-school education; however, the UNDP-sponsored education report found that in the 1996-97 school year, only 55.8 percent of children aged 5 and 6 years attended pre-school, due to increasing explicit and implicit costs of attendance.

The quality of education received by poor students is also worse than that received by the non-poor. The incidence of students not receiving textbooks is approximately twice as high for poor students as compared with non-poor students (Indicator Box 3.11). This difference in receipt of textbooks between poor and non-poor is probably because non-poor parents are more able to buy textbooks for their children, thus ensuring a higher quality of education.[5]

A similar story holds for tertiary entrance rates, where the poor are much less likely to receive education. This is also partly due to the high implicit costs of admittance, due to the prevalence of bribery for entrance examinations and progression within the higher education system. Poor people aged 17-24 years have an enrolment rate of just 14.1 percent—just a third of the enrolment rate of their non-poor counterparts (40.1 percent).

These trends, if continued, would jeopardize the future of Moldova, by ensuring that many of today's poor children would also grow up to face poverty. As discussed in Chapter 1, educational attainment of the household head, and individual education, had a very high correlation to whether someone was non-poor. Thus, the failure to fully educate themselves may place poor children at a definite disadvantage in Moldova's future labor market.

Public resources to significantly increase educational spending is unavailable. Therefore, increasing the efficiency of public education expenditures is of primary importance. This will have to be through a rationalization of the education system, so that the limited public resources are spent efficiently. Thus, the education system will have to be examined and restructured over the longer run, with a focus on decreasing costs through possible consolidation of schools and closing of wings to conserve energy expenses. One method to improve efficiency would be to reduce the numbers of staff (including teachers) while improving the salaries and the morale of those who remain.[6] Public resources will have to be refocused away from tertiary level education to mostly primary and secondary schools, especially in rural areas. Greater cost recovery for higher education, and for optional courses (such as music and languages) at lower education levels, will also release resources that can be best targeted to the poor. Over the longer

---

[5] An issue related to the quality of education is how easy is it for students to reach their schools. Evidence in de Soto and Dudwick (1997) suggests that some students are disadvantaged by having to walk to school during winter and this leads to students missing school.

[6] Unfortunately, there is not any readily available information on changes in student-teacher ratios since independence. However, evidence from de Soto and Dudwick (1997) and the UNDP-sponsored report on education suggests that teachers are already leaving the profession because of low salaries.

time horizon, however, increased incomes, by lowering the opportunity costs to poor households of sending their children to school, will allow them to focus on investing in education rather than on just how to meet consumption needs. To the extent that the reforms are concentrated on the lower levels of the system, it will also be pro-poor, or "broadly targeted" (Tool Box 3.12).

TOOL BOX 3.12: Broad targeting of public expenditures

"Broad Targeting" involves laying emphasis on areas of spending that allocates public expenditures preferably towards areas that are known to disproportionately benefit the poor. Basic social expenditures are a clear example—money spent on primary education is much more likely to reach the poor than money spent on universities, since poor students would have dropped out of the educational system in later stages, unable or unwilling to afford further schooling. For health, spending on health care centers offering basic care have much more of a pro-poor effect than spending on hospitals (van der Walle 1998). Broad targeting, however, may not reach specially vulnerable groups or be able to respond to sudden shocks.

Access to health services

For Governments concerned with alleviating poverty, the promotion of good health becomes of particular importance, since poor health status and poverty are mutually reinforcing. Poor people have lower means and ability to seek proper health care, thus worsening the health of themselves and their family. Worsening health status also makes them less able to find and keep steady, well-paying jobs, which, as discussed in the last chapter, is the surest way of pulling households out of poverty. For Governments, effective spending on better health access for the poor may thus be cost-effective in many ways, not least of which is that it may save on social assistance spending in the future.

In transition economies such as Moldova, there is a need to ensure that the poor have the best access to health care. Given the overall budget constraints, this implies a relative decrease in free access to Government-provided health care for those more able to pay, and a focus on supplying the poor with affordable basic health care.

COMPARATOR BOX 3.13: Between 1992 and 1996, infant mortality in Moldova increased drastically (child deaths per thousand)

| Country | Infant Mortality Rates | | Change |
	1996	1992	in deaths
Tajikistan	31.8	45.9	-31%
Kyrgyz Rep.	25.9	31.5	-18%
Kazakhstan	24.8	26.1	-5%
Moldova	**20.2**	**18.4**	**+10%**
Azerbaijan	19.9	25.5	-22%
Georgia	17.4*	12.4	+40%
Russia	17.0	18.0	-6%
Latvia	15.8	17.4	-9%
Ukraine	14.3	14.0	+2%
Belarus	10.4	12.3	-15%
Estonia	10.4	15.2	-32%
Lithuania	10.0	16.5	-39%

Note: *1996 figure for Georgia is estimated by Kuddo (1998).
Source: CIS STAT (1997), reported in Kuddo (1998), own calculations.

There is strong evidence to suggest that there has been a decline in health status in Moldova since independence. The crude death rate (death rate per 1,000 persons) increased markedly from 9.7 in 1990 to 11.5 in 1996 (this was less than the peak of 12.2 in 1995). The infant mortality rate increased from 19.0 per 1,000 live births in 1990 to 20.2 in 1996 (Comparator Box 3.13). The crude birth rate in Moldova declined from 17.7 per 1,000 persons in 1990 to 12 per 1000 persons in 1996. Life expectancy at birth has also fallen from 67.7 years in 1991 to 65.8 years in 1995 (life expectancy for men has fallen from 64.3 to 61.8 years, while for women the fall has been from 71 to 69.7 years).

The epidemiological situation in Moldova is also a cause for concern. The incidence of tuberculosis rose from 43.8 cases per 100,000 persons in 1991 to 58.7 in 1996. The incidence of hepatitis approximately doubled between 1993 and 1995. However, post-epidemiological transition diseases such as circulatory diseases and malignant neoplasms together were the most important cause of death in Moldova in 1995.[7] Deaths from car accidents increased from 13.3 per 100,000 persons in 1992 to 18.8 in 1995. A major problem for Moldova is the unprecedented increase in the incidence of syphilis from 20.4 cases per 100,000 persons in 1991 to 200.7 in 1996.

The decline in public spending is, once again, a factor in explaining this apparent decline in health status in Moldova. An obvious factor is the decline in public health spending. While public health expenditure as a share of GDP has been constant at around 5 percent of GDP over the period 1991 to 1996, with a shrinking GDP base, the real level of public health resources still contracted over this period. A recent study of the healthcare industry in Moldova[8] confirms this, indicating that the real level of public health expenditures in 1996 was 50 percent of the 1990 level.

At the same time, there have been significant increases in out-of pocket expenses for medical care, resulting in the poor not being able to afford many services. Although the state has officially continued to provide free or low fee medical services, serious shortages of hospital equipment and medicine, low salaries for

✓ INDICATOR BOX 3.14: **The average level of private health care expenditures is much smaller for poor households (percent)**

	Poor	Non-poor	Total
As a share of total household expenditures	1.1	3.1	2.7
As a share of total non-food expenditures	7.5	8.1	8.0
As a share of expenditure of the "non-poor"	12.0	100.0	83.4

Source: Ackland (1997), from Moldova Pilot Survey Data, February 1997.

medical personnel (130-220 lei for doctors), and a long tradition of doctors and nurses demanding and accepting small "gifts" for special attention, have all created what is predominantly a *de facto*, if not *de jure*, system of private medicine. When patients enter the hospital, they must provide everything: bed linens, blankets, food, medicine, even syringes. Patients who enter a hospital in Chisinau for surgery must ask their relatives to bring blood; doctors claim the hospital supplies have been depleted. Alternatively, relatives look for donors whom they must pay to provide blood. As a result, health care has become relatively unaffordable for the poor (Indicator Box 3.14), and the average level of health expenditures for poor households is only 12 percent of that spent by non-poor households.

VOICES: Anonymous Moldovan
"We are ill because of poverty -- poverty is like an illness."
--de Soto and Dudwick (1997)

As with education, a broadly targeted pro-poor health policy would lay more stress on (and provide more expenditures to) primary health care over tertiary care. This may be happening *de facto* in Moldova, as overall health spending shrinks. The percentage of health expenditures devoted to hospital-based health care has decreased each year since 1993. Similarly, over the period 1993 to 1996 the percentage of public health expenditures used for

---

[7] The incidence of malignant tumors is particularly high in the northern region of Moldova; a major contributor to the rise in oncological diseases in Moldova was the Chernobyl catastrophe in 1986.

[8] D. V. Tintiuk, "Accessibility of Healthcare for the Poor," UNDP-sponsored report, 1997.

'public health activities' increased from 11 to 20 percent. Moreover, the survey results indicate a level of private spending sufficient to develop a co-payment system aimed at those able to pay. A second reform would therefore be to legitimize out-of-pocket payments for some services; this would create additional financial resources that can be used to improve access by those who are not able to pay.

Overall, Moldova's health care strategy has to begin by aggressively restructuring the provider network to deploy resources more efficiently, strengthen the primary care network, and formalize the system of unofficial payments for health care while providing a small basic package of health services free of charge to the poor. The hospital network, especially, suffers from over-capacity, and is diverting needed resources from the primary care areas. Over the medium term, the goal would be to drastically reduce hospital capacity in Chisinau, and to keep one hospital per *judet* in the rest of the country. Outpatient facilities such as polyclinics would be either closed or refurbished to house primary care providers. At the same time, the resources released from this would be directed to establish an

---

Pillars of health care reform in Moldova

➢ *Restructuring the over-sized provider network*, to release resources from tertiary-level health care to primary level care.

➢ *Strengthening the primary care network*, through increased resources funding the establishment of an effective network of general practitioners.

➢ *Formalizing the existing informal payments*, to protect payments from arbitrary and excessive health care costs that are especially burdensome for the poor.

➢ *Redefining the basic health care package in line with budgetary resources*, with the majority of resources going towards primary care.

➢ *Centralized funding of health care* to improve the intra-sectoral allocation of resources.

➢ *Organizational reforms to make health service providers financially and managerially autonomous entities* without direct budgetary support.

---

effective framework of general practitioners providing primary care, which is the most essential service accessed by the poor. Allowing some medical personnel to leave for private practice would lower the number of public providers and provide the funds to raise their salaries, which will help to reduce their informal charges and improve quality of care. A basic package of services will be available to all, free of charge. The package, however, will need to be streamlined to cover only the most essential interventions, and the contents of the package will have to be made consistent with available fiscal resources for health care.

Better access by the poor in both health and education will also be helped by improved targeting of benefits to the poor, combined with restructuring of the sectors to improve their efficiency. With no significant increase in the level of social sector expenditure expected in the near future, there is a need to both increase the use of private funds from those who can afford it, and to improve the efficiency with which the funds are used. For both education and health care, the survey indicates that there is the willingness and ability of many households to increase their own contributions. In health care, there is already a level of private spending that is sufficient to cover co-payments for those most capable of payment. Similarly, education offers some possibilities for cost recovery. Over 70 percent of households on the Right Bank indicated their willingness to buy textbooks for their children, if this would improve the quality of education. There may also be scope to introduce fees for extra-curricular courses in specialized secondary and tertiary education. Once again, essential services need to be provided at low or no cost to the poor, and this requires the development of a better system to identify the poorest.

Once again, income growth and its distribution will be the key influences on both education and health status in the long-run. Increased incomes will allow households to purchase more health care and education services. Increased government revenue, in turn, will expand the opportunity for public provision of primary education and preventative and curative health services.

Moldova's Government, therefore, faces a critical challenge—how to protect the population today while laying the foundations for a better tomorrow. It will only be able to achieve this if it can take bold and far-sighted reforms that stop the wastage of scarce financial resources, provide the current generation with social support that is equitable and fair, and transform the macro-labor economic environment to one that supports increased incomes for all.

REFERENCES

Ackland, Robert (1998). "Poverty in the Republic of Moldova in May and August 1997," in World Bank (1999).

Ackland, Robert (1997). "Human Capital and Poverty in the Republic of Moldova," in World Bank (1999).

Atkinson, Anthony (1995). "On targeting social security: Theory and Western Experience with Family Benefits," in Dominique van de Walle and Kimberly Nead, eds., *Public Spending and the Poor: Theory and Evidence,* Johns Hopkins University Press, Baltimore, pp. 25-68.

Allison, Christine and Dena Ringold (1996). *Labor Markets in Transition in Central and Eastern Europe.* World Bank Technical Paper No. 352, The World Bank, Washington DC.

Braithwaite, Jeanine (1997a). "Poverty in Moldova: Pilot Results for February 1997," in World Bank (1999).

Braithwaite, Jeanine (1997b). "General Concepts for Proxy Means Testing," World Bank, Washington, D.C. Mimeo.

De Soto, Hermine and Nora Dudwick (1997). "Poverty in Moldova: A Qualitative Study," in World Bank (1999).

Heleniak, T. (1996). "Migration and population change in the Soviet successor states." Paper presented at National convention of American Association for the Advancement of Slavic Studies, Boston, Mass., November 14-17. Mimeo.

Kuddo, Arvo (1998): "Social Transition: Social and Employment Policies in the Former Soviet Union States." Europe and Central Asia Region, The World Bank. Mimeo.

Lerman, Zvi, Csaba Csaki and Victor Moroz (1998): *Land Reform and Farm Restructuring in Moldova.* World Bank Discussion Paper No. 398, The World Bank, Washington DC.

Lindauer, David (1998): "Labor and Poverty in the Republic of Moldova," in World Bank (1999).

Ravallion, Martin (1999): "Appraising Workfare," *World Bank Research Observer*, Vol. 14, No. 1, pp. 31-48.

Sandu, Maya (1999): "Energy: Privileges and Compensations," World Bank Resident Mission in Moldova. Mimeo.

Tuck, Laura and Kathy Lindert (1996): *From Universal Food Subsidies to a Self-Targeted Program: A Case Study in Tunisian Reform.* World Bank Discussion Paper No. 351, The World Bank, Washington DC.

UNDP (1995). *Human Development Report.* Oxford University Press. New York, New York, USA.

Van de Walle, Dominique (1998): "Targeting Revisited," *World Bank Research Observer,* Vol. 13, No. 2, pp. 231-48.

Van de Walle, Dominique (1995): "Incidence and Targeting: An overview of the implications for research and policy", in Dominique van de Walle and Kimberly Nead, eds., *Public Spending and the Poor: Theory and Evidence,* Johns Hopkins University Press, Baltimore, pp. 585-619.

World Bank (1999): "Moldova: Poverty Assessment Technical Papers," Report No. 19846 MD. The World Bank. Washington DC.

World Bank (1992, 1993, 1997): *World Development Report.* Johns Hopkins University Press. Baltimore, Maryland, USA.

Distributors of World Bank Group Publications

Prices and credit terms vary from country to country. Consult your local distributor before placing an order.

ARGENTINA
World Publications SA
Av. Cordoba 1877
1120 Ciudad de Buenos Aires
Tel: (54 11) 4815-8156
Fax: (54 11) 4815-8156
E-mail: wpbooks@infovia.com.ar

AUSTRALIA, FIJI, PAPUA NEW GUINEA, SOLOMON ISLANDS, VANUATU, AND SAMOA
D.A. Information Services
648 Whitehorse Road
Mitcham 3132, Victoria
Tel: (61) 3 9210 7777
Fax: (61) 3 9210 7788
E-mail: service@dadirect.com.au
URL: http://www.dadirect.com.au

AUSTRIA
Gerold and Co.
Weihburggasse 26
A-1011 Wien
Tel: (43 1) 512-47-31-0
Fax: (43 1) 512-47-31-29
URL: http://www.gerold.co/at.online

BANGLADESH
Micro Industries Development
Assistance Society (MIDAS)
House 5, Road 16
Dhanmondi R/Area
Dhaka 1209
Tel: (880 2) 326427
Fax: (880 2) 811188

BELGIUM
Jean De Lannoy
Av. du Roi 202
1060 Brussels
Tel: (32 2) 538-5169
Fax: (32 2) 538-0841

BRAZIL
Publicacões Tecnicas Internacionais Ltda.
Rua Peixoto Gomide, 209
01409 Sao Paulo, SP.
Tel: (55 11) 259-6644
Fax: (55 11) 258-6990
E-mail: postmaster@pti.uol.br
URL: http://www.uol.br

CANADA
Renouf Publishing Co. Ltd.
5369 Canotek Road
Ottawa, Ontario K1J 9J3
Tel: (613) 745-2665
Fax: (613) 745-7660
E-mail: order.dept@renoufbooks.com
URL: http:// www.renoufbooks.com

CHINA
China Financial & Economic
Publishing House
8, Da Fo Si Dong Jie
Beijing
Tel: (86 10) 6401-7365
Fax: (86 10) 6401-7365

China Book Import Centre
P.O. Box 2825
Beijing

Chinese Corporation for Promotion
of Humanities
52, You Fang Hu Tong,
Xuan Nei Da Jie
Beijing
Tel: (86 10) 660 72 494
Fax: (86 10) 660 72 494

COLOMBIA
Infoenlace Ltda.
Carrera 6 No. 51-21
Apartado Aereo 34270
Santafé de Bogotá, D.C.
Tel: (57 1) 285-2798
Fax: (57 1) 285-2798

COTE D'IVOIRE
Center d'Edition et de Diffusion
Africaines (CEDA)
04 B.P. 541
Abidjan 04
Tel: (225) 24 6510; 24 6511
Fax: (225) 25 0567

CYPRUS
Center for Applied Research
Cyprus College
6, Diogenes Street, Engomi
P.O. Box 2006
Nicosia
Tel: (357 2) 59-0730
Fax: (357 2) 66-2051

CZECH REPUBLIC
USIS, NIS Prodejna
Havelkova 22
130 00 Prague 3
Tel: (420 2) 2423 1486
Fax: (420 2) 2423 1114
URL: http://www.nis.cz/

DENMARK
SamfundsLitteratur
Rosenoerns Allé 11
DK-1970 Frederiksberg C
Tel: (45 35) 351942
Fax: (45 35) 357822
URL: http://www.sl.cbs.dk

ECUADOR
Libri Mundi
Libreria Internacional
P.O. Box 17-01-3029
Juan Leon Mera 851
Quito
Tel: (593 2) 521-606; (593 2) 544-185
Fax: (593 2) 504-209
E-mail: librimu1@librimundi.com.ec
E-mail: librimu2@librimundi.com.ec

CODEU
Ruiz de Castilla 763, Edif. Expocolor
Primer piso, Of. #2
Quito
Tel/Fax: (593 2) 507-383; 253-091
E-mail: codeu@impsat.net.ec

EGYPT, ARAB REPUBLIC OF
Al Ahram Distribution Agency
Al Galaa Street
Cairo
Tel: (20 2) 578-6083
Fax: (20 2) 578-6833

The Middle East Observer
41, Sherif Street
Cairo
Tel: (20 2) 393-9732
Fax: (20 2) 393-9732

FINLAND
Akateeminen Kirjakauppa
P.O. Box 128
FIN-00101 Helsinki
Tel: (358 0) 121 4418
Fax: (358 0) 121-4435
E-mail: akatilaus@stockmann.fi
URL: http://www.akateeminen.com

FRANCE
Editions Eska; DBJ
48, rue Gay Lussac
75005 Paris
Tel: (33-1) 55-42-73-08
Fax: (33-1) 43-29-91-67

GERMANY
UNO-Verlag
Poppelsdorfer Allee 55
53115 Bonn
Tel: (49 228) 949020
Fax: (49 228) 217492
URL: http://www.uno-verlag.de
E-mail: unoverlag@aol.com

GHANA
Epp Books Services
P.O. Box 44
TUC
Accra
Tel: 223 21 778843
Fax: 223 21 779099

GREECE
Papasotiriou S.A.
35, Stournara Str.
106 82 Athens
Tel: (30 1) 364-1826
Fax: (30 1) 364-8254

HAITI
Culture Diffusion
5, Rue Capois
C.P. 257
Port-au-Prince
Tel: (509) 23 9260
Fax: (509) 23 4858

HONG KONG, CHINA; MACAO
Asia 2000 Ltd.
Sales & Circulation Department
302 Seabird House
22-28 Wyndham Street, Central
Hong Kong, China
Tel: (852) 2530-1409
Fax: (852) 2526-1107
E-mail: sales@asia2000.com.hk
URL: http://www.asia2000.com.hk

HUNGARY
Euro Info Service
Margitszgeti Europa Haz
H-1138 Budapest
Tel: (36 1) 350 80 24, 350 80 25
Fax: (36 1) 350 90 32
E-mail: euroinfo@mail.matav.hu

INDIA
Allied Publishers Ltd.
751 Mount Road
Madras - 600 002
Tel: (91 44) 852-3938
Fax: (91 44) 852-0649

INDONESIA
Pt. Indira Limited
Jalan Borobudur 20
P.O. Box 181
Jakarta 10320
Tel: (62 21) 390-4290
Fax: (62 21) 390-4289

IRAN
Ketab Sara Co. Publishers
Khaled Eslamboli Ave., 6th Street
Delafrooz Alley No. 8
P.O. Box 15745-733
Tehran 15117
Tel: (98 21) 8717819; 8716104
Fax: (98 21) 8712479
E-mail: ketab-sara@neda.net.ir

Kowkab Publishers
P.O. Box 19575-511
Tehran
Tel: (98 21) 258-3723
Fax: (98 21) 258-3723

IRELAND
Government Supplies Agency
Oifig an tSoláthair
4-5 Harcourt Road
Dublin 2
Tel: (353 1) 661-3111
Fax: (353 1) 475-2670

ISRAEL
Yozmot Literature Ltd.
P.O. Box 56055
3 Yohanan Hasandlar Street
Tel Aviv 61560
Tel: (972 3) 5285-397
Fax: (972 3) 5285-397

R.O.Y. International
PO Box 13056
Tel Aviv 61130
Tel: (972 3) 649 9469
Fax: (972 3) 648 6039
E-mail: royil@netvision.net.il
URL: http://www.royint.co.il

Palestinian Authority/Middle East
Index Information Services
P.O.B. 19502 Jerusalem
Tel: (972 2) 6271219
Fax: (972 2) 6271634

ITALY, LIBERIA
Licosa Commissionaria Sansoni SPA
Via Duca Di Calabria, 1/1
Casella Postale 552
50125 Firenze
Tel: (39 55) 645-415
Fax: (39 55) 641-257
E-mail: licosa@ftbcc.it
URL: http://www.ftbcc.it/licosa

JAMAICA
Ian Randle Publishers Ltd.
206 Old Hope Road, Kingston 6
Tel: 876-927-2085
Fax: 876-977-0243
E-mail: irpl@colis.com

JAPAN
Eastern Book Service
3-13 Hongo 3-chome, Bunkyo-ku
Tokyo 113
Tel: (81 3) 3818-0861
Fax: (81 3) 3818-0864
E-mail: orders@svt-ebs.co.jp
URL: http://www.bekkoame.or.jp/~svt-ebs

KENYA
Africa Book Service (E.A.) Ltd.
Quaran House, Mfangano Street
P.O. Box 45245
Nairobi
Tel: (254 2) 223 641
Fax: (254 2) 330 272

Legacy Books
Loita House
Mezzanine 1
P.O. Box 68077
Nairobi
Tel: (254) 2-330853, 221426
Fax: (254) 2-330854, 561654
E-mail: Legacy@form-net.com

KOREA, REPUBLIC OF
Dayang Books Trading Co.
International Division
783-20, Pangba Bon-Dong,
Socho-ku
Seoul
Tel: (82 2) 536-9555
Fax: (82 2) 536-0025
E-mail: seamap@chollian.net

Eulyoo Publishing Co., Ltd.
46-1, Susong-Dong
Jongro-Gu
Seoul
Tel: (82 2) 734-3515
Fax: (82 2) 732-9154

LEBANON
Librairie du Liban
P.O. Box 11-9232
Beirut
Tel: (961 9) 217 944
Fax: (961 9) 217 434
E-mail: hsayegh@librairie-du-liban.com.lb
URL: http://www.librairie-du-liban.com.lb

MALAYSIA
University of Malaya Cooperative
Bookshop, Limited
P.O. Box 1127
Jalan Pantai Baru
59700 Kuala Lumpur
Tel: (60 3) 756-5000
Fax: (60 3) 755-4424
E-mail: umkoop@tm.net.my

MEXICO
INFOTEC
Av. San Fernando No. 37
Col. Toriello Guerra
14050 Mexico, D.F.
Tel: (52 5) 624-2800
Fax: (52 5) 624-2822
E-mail: infotec@rtn.net.mx
URL: http://rtn.net.mx

Mundi-Prensa Mexico S.A. de C.V.
c/Rio Panuco, 141-Colonia
Cuauhtemoc
06500 Mexico, D.F.
Tel: (52 5) 533-5658
Fax: (52 5) 514-6799

NEPAL
Everest Media International Services
(P.) Ltd.
GPO Box 5443
Kathmandu
Tel: (977 1) 416 026
Fax: (977 1) 224 431

NETHERLANDS
De Lindeboom/Internationale
Publicaties b.v.-
P.O. Box 202, 7480 AE Haaksbergen
Tel: (31 53) 574-0004
Fax: (31 53) 572-9296
E-mail: lindeboo@worldonline.nl
URL: http://www.worldonline.nl/~lin-deboo

NEW ZEALAND
EBSCO NZ Ltd.
Private Mail Bag 99914
New Market
Auckland
Tel: (64 9) 524-8119
Fax: (64 9) 524-8067

Oasis Official
P.O. Box 3627
Wellington
Tel: (64 4) 499 1551
Fax: (64 4) 499 1972
E-mail: oasis@actrix.gen.nz
URL: http://www.oasisbooks.co.nz/

NIGERIA
University Press Limited
Three Crowns Building Jericho
Private Mail Bag 5095
Ibadan
Tel: (234 22) 41-1356
Fax: (234 22) 41-2056

PAKISTAN
Mirza Book Agency
65, Shahrah-e-Quaid-e-Azam
Lahore 54000
Tel: (92 42) 735 3601
Fax: (92 42) 576 3714

Oxford University Press
5 Bangalore Town
Sharae Faisal
PO Box 13033
Karachi-75350
Tel: (92 21) 446307
Fax: (92 21) 4547640
E-mail: ouppak@TheOffice.net

Pak Book Corporation
Aziz Chambers 21, Queen's Road
Lahore
Tel: (92 42) 636 3222; 636 0885
Fax: (92 42) 636 2328
E-mail: pbc@brain.net.pk

PERU
Editorial Desarrollo SA
Apartado 3824, Ica 242 OF. 106
Lima 1
Tel: (51 14) 285380
Fax: (51 14) 286628

PHILIPPINES
International Booksource Center Inc.
1127-A Antipolo St, Barangay,
Venezuela
Makati City
Tel: (63 2) 896 6501; 6505; 6507
Fax: (63 2) 896 1741

POLAND
International Publishing Service
Ul. Piekna 31/37
00-677 Warzawa
Tel: (48 2) 628-6089
Fax: (48 2) 621-7255
E-mail: books%ips@ikp.atm.com.pl
URL: http://www.ipscg.waw.pl/ips/export

PORTUGAL
Livraria Portugal
Apartado 2681, Rua Do Carm
o 70-74
1200 Lisbon
Tel: (1) 347-4982
Fax: (1) 347-0264

ROMANIA
Compani De Librarii Bucuresti S.A.
Str. Lipscani no. 26, sector 3
Bucharest
Tel: (40 1) 313 9645
Fax: (40 1) 312 4000

RUSSIAN FEDERATION
Isdatelstvo <Ves Mir>
9a, Kolpachniy Pereulok
Moscow 101831
Tel: (7 095) 917 87 49
Fax: (7 095) 917 92 59
ozimarin@glasnet.ru

SINGAPORE; TAIWAN, CHINA
MYANMAR; BRUNEI
Hemisphere Publication Services
41 Kallang Pudding Road #04-03
Golden Wheel Building
Singapore 349316
Tel: (65) 741-5166
Fax: (65) 742-9356
E-mail: ashgate@asianconnect.com

SLOVENIA
Gospodarski vestnik Publishing
Group
Dunajska cesta 5
1000 Ljubljana
Tel: (386 61) 133 83 47; 132 12 30
Fax: (386 61) 133 80 30
E-mail: repansekj@gvestnik.si

SOUTH AFRICA, BOTSWANA
For single titles:
Oxford University Press Southern
Africa
Vasco Boulevard, Goodwood
P.O. Box 12119, N1 City 7463
Cape Town
Tel: (27 21) 595 4400
Fax: (27 21) 595 4430
E-mail: oxford@oup.co.za

For subscription orders:
International Subscription Service
P.O. Box 41095
Craighall
Johannesburg 2024
Tel: (27 11) 880-1448
Fax: (27 11) 880-6248
E-mail: iss@is.co.za

SPAIN
Mundi-Prensa Libros, S.A.
Castello 37
28001 Madrid
Tel: (34 91) 4 363700
Fax: (34 91) 5 753998
E-mail: libreria@mundiprensa.es
URL: http://www.mundiprensa.com/

Mundi-Prensa Barcelona
Consell de Cent, 391
08009 Barcelona
Tel: (34 3) 488-3492
Fax: (34 3) 487-7659
E-mail: barcelona@mundiprensa.es

SRI LANKA, THE MALDIVES
Lake House Bookshop
100, Sir Chittampalam Gardiner
Mawatha
Colombo 2
Tel: (94 1) 32105
Fax: (94 1) 432104
E-mail: LHL@sri.lanka.net

SWEDEN
Wennergren-Williams AB
P. O. Box 1305
S-171 25 Solna
Tel: (46 8) 705-97-50
Fax: (46 8) 27-00-71
E-mail: mail@wwi.se

SWITZERLAND
Librairie Payot Service Institutionnel
C(tm)tes-de-Montbenon 30
1002 Lausanne
Tel: (41 21) 341-3229
Fax: (41 21) 341-3235

ADECO Van Diermen
EditionsTechniques
Ch. de Lacuez 41
CH1807 Blonay
Tel: (41 21) 943 2673
Fax: (41 21) 943 3605

THAILAND
Central Books Distribution
306 Silom Road
Bangkok 10500
Tel: (66 2) 2336930-9
Fax: (66 2) 237-8321

TRINIDAD & TOBAGO
AND THE CARRIBBEAN
Systematics Studies Ltd.
St. Augustine Shopping Center
Eastern Main Road, St. Augustine
Trinidad & Tobago, West Indies
Tel: (868) 645-8466
Fax: (868) 645-8467
E-mail: tobe@trinidad.net

UGANDA
Gustro Ltd.
PO Box 9997, Madhvani Building
Plot 16/4 Jinja Rd.
Kampala
Tel: (256 41) 251 467
Fax: (256 41) 251 468
E-mail: gus@swiftuganda.com

UNITED KINGDOM
Microinfo Ltd.
P.O. Box 3, Omega Park, Alton,
Hampshire GU34 2PG
England
Tel: (44 1420) 86848
Fax: (44 1420) 89889
E-mail: wbank@microinfo.co.uk
URL: http://www.microinfo.co.uk

The Stationery Office
51 Nine Elms Lane
London SW8 5DR
Tel: (44 171) 873-8400
Fax: (44 171) 873-8242
URL: http://www.the-stationery-office.co.uk/

VENEZUELA
Tecni-Ciencia Libros, S.A.
Centro Cuidad Comercial Tamanco
Nivel C2, Caracas
Tel: (58 2) 959 5547; 5035; 0016
Fax: (58 2) 959 5636

ZAMBIA
University Bookshop, University of
Zambia
Great East Road Campus
P.O. Box 32379
Lusaka
Tel: (260 1) 252 576
Fax: (260 1) 253 952

ZIMBABWE
Academic and Baobab Books (Pvt.)
Ltd.
4 Conald Road, Graniteside
P.O. Box 567
Harare
Tel: 263 4 755035
Fax: 263 4 781913

MAP SECTION

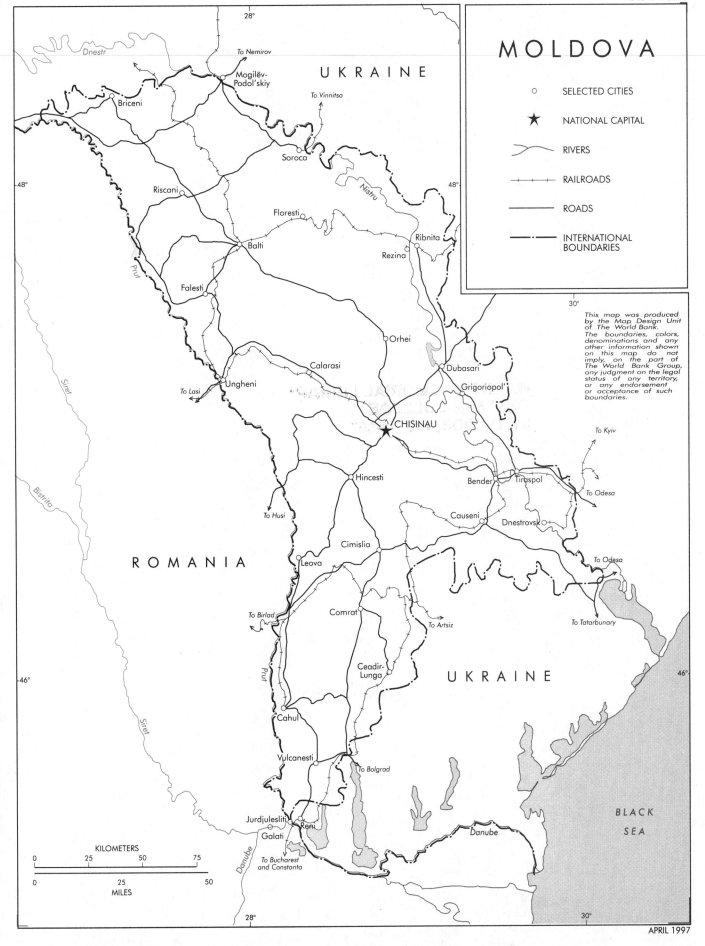

IBRD 24285R3

MOLDOVA

○ SELECTED CITIES

★ NATIONAL CAPITAL

〜 RIVERS

+|+|+ RAILROADS

── ROADS

─·─·─ INTERNATIONAL BOUNDARIES

This map was produced by the Map Design Unit of The World Bank.
The boundaries, colors, denominations and any other information shown on this map do not imply, on the part of The World Bank Group, any judgment on the legal status of any territory, or any endorsement or acceptance of such boundaries.

UKRAINE

Dnestr

To Nemirov

Mogilëv-Podol'skiy

To Vinnitsa

Briceni

Soroca

Nistru

Riscani

48°   48°

Floresti

Ribnita

Balti

Rezina

Prut

Falesti

Orhei

Dubasari

Calarasi

Grigoriopol

To Lasi

Ungheni

CHISINAU

To Kyiv

Hincesti

Bender   Tiraspol

To Odesa

Causeni

Dnestrovsk

To Husi

ROMANIA

Cimislia

Leova

To Odesa

Siret

To Birlad

Comrat

To Artsiz

To Tatarbunary

Bistrita

Ceadir-Lunga

UKRAINE

46°   46°

Cahul

Prut

Siret

Vulcanesti

To Bolgrad

BLACK SEA

Jurdjulesliti   Reni

Galati

Danube

Danube

To Bucharest and Constanta

KILOMETERS
0   25   50   75

0   25   50
MILES

28°   30°

APRIL 1997